....
I'LL START, THEN.
MM...
THAT'S NOT FAIR, MAKOTO-CHAN!
I GET TO GO FIRST!
!
WHAT ARE YOU TWO...?
...AH.
YOU'RE AWAKE, SOU-CHAN?
SOU-CHAN...
TAKA-TSUKI-KUN...

WHICH OF US DO YOU WANT TO DO IT WITH?
GABA (JUMP)
J-JUST A DREAM!?

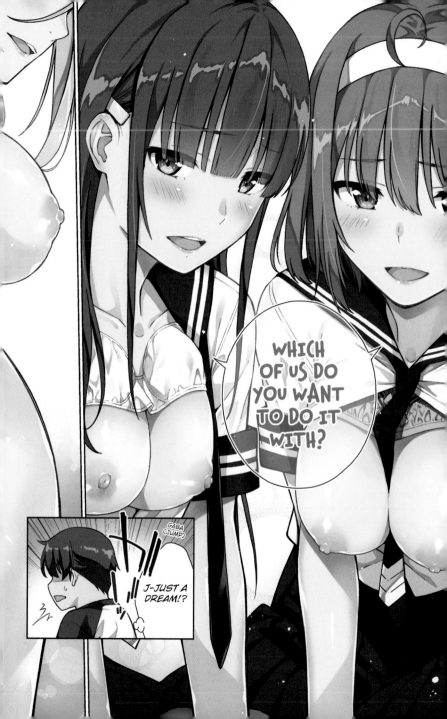

Chapter 12

LVST GEASS

Osamu Takahashi

Lust Geass

[3]

contents

THAT DAY, AFTER SCHOOL ...
HERE, TAKATSUKI-KUN.
YOU DROPPED THIS YESTERDAY, DIDN'T YOU?
OH... THIS.
THE COPY I RETURNED TO USUI...
...TAKATSUKI-KUN.
SIGN: FACULTY ROOM
......
DID SOMETHING HAPPEN BETWEEN YOU AND USUI-SAN YESTERDAY?
職員室
EH!?
NO... I MEAN...
NOTHING SPECIAL...

...I SEE.
I DON'T INTEND TO MEDDLE IN STUDENTS' ROMANTIC AFFAIRS...
...BUT YOU SHOULD NEVER DO ANYTHING THAT WOULD MAKE A GIRL CRY.
R-RIGHT.
YOUR FRIENDS ARE HERE...
...SO YOU CAN GO.
PON (PAT)
SOU-CHAN!
ARE YOU DONE?
HERE'S YOUR BAG.
LET'S GO HOME.
TH-THANKS.

HUH? IS THAT THE BOOK I LENT YOU?
DID SENSEI WANT TO TALK TO YOU ABOUT THAT?
DOKI (THUMP)
UM... I GUESS I FORGOT IT IN THE CLASSROOM YESTERDAY, AND SENSEI HELD ON TO IT FOR ME...
EH...? DID SHE LOOK INSIDE?
NO... I DON'T THINK SO.
OKAY...
Usui... This is actually yours.
You must've dropped it yesterday.
HISO (WHISPER)
HISO
Oh... It must've been when I collided with Sensei.
I'll give it back to you later.
SOU-CHAN, MAKOTO-CHAN IS COMING OVER TODAY TO BORROW SOME MANGA...
...BUT SHE ALSO SAID SHE WANTS TO SEE YOUR ROOM.

EH...? MY ROOM?
I DON'T GET THE CHANCE TO SEE A BOY'S BEDROOM EVERY DAY.
IT'S FINE IF I'M WITH RIKKA, ISN'T IT?
IT'S FINE! I JUST CLEANED IT FOR HIM TOO.
RIKKA... IT'S NOT FOR YOU TO DECIDE.
TAKATSUKI-KUN...DOESN'T SEEM TO HAVE BROKEN UP WITH AMANOME-SAN.
AND YET, HE WAS LIKE THAT WITH USUI-SAN...
I'M SUR-PRISED...
...BY USUI-SAN'S BEHAVIOR TOO.
AH...
RIKKA...
EVEN THOUGH USUI JUST LEFT...
MUNI (GROPE)
MUNYU (SQUISH)
NYUCHI (SQUEEZE)

I MEAN... I CAN'T HOLD BACK.
AND LATELY, WE HAVEN'T BEEN DOING IT AS OFTEN AS BEFORE.
KUNYU (RUB)
KUNYU
MUNYU
HUFF HUFF...
HOW'S THIS?
DOES IT FEEL GOOD...?
HUFF HUFF...♥
...SOU-CHAN?
HUFF HUFF! HUFF HUFF!
RIKKA...
I'M ABOUT TO BLOW...
DOPU (SPLURT)
AH...

PERO (LICK)
SOU-CHAN'S STUFF... GOT ALL OVER MY FACE.
HUFF...
I'D BETTER TAKE A SHOWER WHEN I GET HOME.
WELL, SEE YOU LATER, SOU-CHAN.
YEAH.
WHEW...
SU (RUSTLE)
...I COULD HEAR YOU TWO FROM THE OTHER ROOM.
IF YOUR MOM HAD BEEN HOME, YOU GUYS WOULD HAVE BEEN BUSTED.

WE TRY TO BE QUIET WHEN SHE IS HOME...
HUH... SO YOU EVEN DO IT WHEN SHE'S HOME.
LUCKY RIKKA.
USUI...
IS THIS THE REASON YOU WANTED TO VISIT MY ROOM?
"MAKOTO."
YOU PROMISED TO CALL ME THAT WHEN WE'RE ALONE, REMEMBER?
......
I LIKE DOING IT WITH YOU, SOUTA-KUN...
...BUT I LIKE WATCHING YOU DO IT WITH RIKKA JUST ABOUT AS MUCH.
BECAUSE IT LETS ME RECONFIRM...
...JUST HOW IMMORAL MY ACTIONS ARE.

MAKO-TO...
I NEVER KNEW YOU WERE LIKE THIS.
NEITHER DID I.
YOU MADE ME REALIZE IT, SOUTA-KUN.
W-WAIT.
WE DON'T HAVE MUCH TIME BEFORE MY MOM COMES HOME.
DON'T WORRY. I HAVE A CURFEW TOO.
JUST GIVE ME A TASTE TODAY.
SINCE THEN...
...MY DAYS OF DOING IT WITH RIKKA AND THEN USUI CONTINUED.
SUPPOSEDLY, DRINKING MY CUM WOULD KEEP THEIR FITS OF HORNINESS UNDER CONTROL, TO AN EXTENT...
...BUT I FOUND MYSELF DOING IT WITH THEM IN PLACES OTHER THAN HOME AND SCHOOL ON A NEAR-DAILY BASIS.

I WAS ESPECIALLY CAREFUL WHEN I DID IT WITH USUI.
I COULDN'T LET RIKKA FIND OUT ABOUT OUR RELATION-SHIP.
AND YET, USUI KEPT COMING OVER TO MY HOUSE...
?
...AND WOULD SEDUCE ME WHENEVER THE THREE OF US WOULD GO OUT.
IT WAS LIKE SHE GOT OFF ON THE THRILL THAT RIKKA MIGHT CATCH US.

EVERY TIME I DID IT WITH USUI, I WOULD FEEL GUILTY ABOUT RIKKA...
...BUT THEN IT FELT SO GOOD THAT ANY GUILT WAS SWEPT AWAY.
AND YET... THE GUILT WOULD ALWAYS RETURN, LIKE A THORN STABBING ME DEEP IN THE HEART.
LIKE THAT...
...THOSE DAYS CONTINUED FOR A WHILE.
UNTIL JULY WAS JUST BEGINNING...
SENSEI!
SHINO-SENSEIIII!
NONE OF THAT!
IT'S "TATEAKI-SENSEI," REMEMBER?
BUT "SHINO-SENSEI" IS CUTER!

BUT...

ANYWAY, SENSEI, WOULD YOU GIVE HER ADVICE?

IT'S FINE! SENSEI GAVE ME ADVICE BEFORE TOO, AND IT WAS REALLY HELPFUL.

GO AHEAD, YUI.

"YOU SHOULD NEVER DO ANYTHING THAT WOULD MAKE A GIRL CRY."

SEN-SEI?

......

AH... SOU-CHAN, DON'T WALK SO FAST...

SUTA
スタ

SUTA
スタ
(TROT)

15

図書室
SIGN: SCHOOL LIBRARY
COME ON, SOU-CHAN, GET OUT YOUR TEXT-BOOK AND NOTES.
TODAY'S STUDY SESSION IS FOR YOU.
YEAH, YEAH...
WE'VE GOT FINALS COMING UP.
I CAN HELP YOU STUDY AT HOME, BUT SCIENCE IS MAKOTO-CHAN'S SPECIALTY.
AH... I'M GOING TO THE WASH-ROOM.
SEE YOU IN A BIT.
LET'S GET STARTED.
USUI...
THAT ASIDE...
THAT ASIDE?
YOU WANT TO DO IT... HERE?
ス
SU (RUSTLE)
BIKUN (TWITCH)

NOT THAT...
I MEAN, IT'S ABOUT THAT, BUT...
AT THIS RATE, I HAVE A FEELING RIKKA'S GOING TO FIND OUT EVENTUALLY...
...SO... HOW ABOUT WE ONLY DO IT WHEN WE'RE ALONE ON THE WEEKENDS?
NO WAY.
TO BE HONEST, EVEN NOW, I'M NOT GETTING ENOUGH.
I'D LIKE TO DO IT EVERY DAY.
I... I CAN'T DO THAT.
I MEAN, I'VE GOT RIKKA ...

JUST MAKE SURE YOU'RE GIVING IT TO HER ENOUGH.

I'LL GET BY SOMEHOW.

...OKAY. YOU WIN.

I'M THE ONE WHO TOLD YOU TO PUT RIKKA FIRST ANYWAY.

TEXTBOOK: MATHEMATICS

I'M BACK...

...I KNOW.

SORRY, RIKKA. WE STARTED CHATTING.

GEEZ... WHAT ARE YOU DOING!?

ANYWAY, LET'S HIT THE BOOKS.

S-SORRY.

SOU-CHAN, YOU HAVEN'T EVEN OPENED YOUR BOOK YET.

...HUH?

GIKU (GULP)

18

AND SO...
DAY TWO OF ABSTINENCE
NOW...
...FROM THAT, WE MAY CONCLUDE...
DAY THREE
OKAY, USUI, TAKE THE NEXT ONE.
USUI ...?
MOJI (FIDGET)
もじ
MOJI
もじ
DAY FIVE
USUI-SAN... ARE YOU OKAY?
DO YOU WANT TO GO TO THE NURSE'S OFFICE?
KUTAA (DROOP)
くたぁ
HUFF...
HUFF...
TAKATSUKI-KUN!!
GA (GRAB)
PLEASE...
I CAN'T HOLD OUT ANY LONGER...
HUFF
HUFF!

LOOK, RIGHT NOW, IT'S FRIDAY, AFTER SCHOOL...

THAT'S PRACTICALLY THE WEEKEND.

NOT REALLY...

I CAN'T...

I CAN'T WAIT...

USUI, WAIT...

TOMORROW'S SATURDAY, SO IF YOU CAN WAIT 'TIL THEN...

MM...

KUCHU (SLURP)

KUCHU

AHHH...

HUFF...

NUCHU (SQUISH)

JURU (DRIBBLE)

MM...

...

WHAT DO YOU THINK? SHOULD WE DO IT HERE?

OR...

AH...

USUI... IF YOU SUCK IT LIKE THAT...

MM...

...AS WE DID IT...

...OVER AND OVER.

USUI WAS MORE INTENSE THAN EVER...

...AH.
THIS LATE ALREADY?
SORRY, TAKATSUKI-KUN. I HAVE TO GO NOW IF I'M GOING TO BE HOME BY CURFEW.
BOOO (DAZED)
OH... SURE.
I'M LOOKING FORWARD TO...
...TOMORROW TOO.
...EH?
W-WAIT A SECOND. I THOUGHT THIS COVERED FOR TOMOR-ROW.
TODAY'S TODAY.
TOMOR-ROW'S A NEW DAY.
......

... UNREAL.

THAT'S WHAT I SAID...

...BUT PART OF ME LOVED DOING IT WITH USUI.

GUESS I'LL GO GET MY BAG.

"YOU ARE NOW CURSED TO DIE THE MOMENT YOU HAVE SEXUAL INTER-COURSE...

"...WITH THE PERSON YOU LOVE THE MOST."

RIGHT NOW, WHICH OF THEM...

...DO I LOVE MORE?

OH, FOR PETE'S SAKE...
WHERE DID IT GO...?
SEN-SEI?
WHAT'S WRONG?
THAT VOICE...
TAKA-TSUKI-KUN?
WHAT ARE YOU STILL DOING HERE? ALL THE OTHER STUDENTS HAVE GONE HOME.
I WAS JUST ABOUT TO LEAVE.
BUT ARE YOU HAVING TROUBLE?
ACTUALLY... I DROPPED SOME PRINT-OUTS...
...AND WHEN I WENT TO PICK THEM UP, I SLIPPED ON ONE AND FELL.
THE MOMENT I HIT THE FLOOR, ONE OF MY CONTACTS POPPED OUT...
IS SHE A KLUTZ...?

I'LL HELP YOU, SENSEI.
EH...? BUT...
...IT'S ALREADY SO LATE...
I CAN'T JUST LEAVE YOU LIKE THIS.
BUT I'M SURPRISED. I NEVER IMAGINED YOU AS BEING THE CLUMSY TYPE.
SUR-PRISED ...?
I HAVE MY MISHAPS ONCE IN A WHILE.
ALL RIGHT. WOULD YOU PICK UP THE PRINTOUTS, THEN?
AH.
I DON'T KNOW WHERE MY CONTACT WENT, SO BE CAREFUL.
OKAY.

MMM... WE'RE JUST NOT FINDING IT.
ARE YOU SURE?
OH WELL. I GIVE UP.
I HAVE A PAIR OF GLASSES IN THE FACULTY ROOM, SO I'LL USE THEM FOR TODAY.
THANK YOU, TAKATSUKI-KUN.
NO, I WASN'T REALLY OF ANY HELP.
YOU'RE KIND.
MAYBE THAT'S THE SECRET TO YOUR POPULARITY.
EH ...!?
I'M NOT ESPE-CIALLY POPULAR ...
BUT LET ME GIVE YOU A WARNING.
DON'T MISTAKE KINDNESS FOR INDECI-SIVENESS.

O-OKAY.
HEH HEH.
IF YOU EVER HAVE A PROBLEM, YOU CAN COME TO ME FOR ADVICE.
THAT'S HOW I CAN THANK YOU FOR—
PAKI (CRACK)
...EH?
TH-THAT CRACKING SOUND ...
DID I STEP ON MY CONTACT...!?
SENSEI, CALM DOWN.
ATA (FRET)
FUTA (PANIC)
あた
ふた
ZURU (SLIP)
SENSEI...!!
DOSA (WHUMP)

OW...
SENSEI, ARE YOU ALL RIGHT?
EH ...?
AH!
YOUR PAPERS ...
GOOD. THEY DIDN'T SCATTER.
ARE YOU HURT?
SENSEI ?
I-I'M FINE!
TA (TAP) TA
GO HOME ALREADY, TAKATSUKI-KUN!
R-RIGHT.

Chapter 13

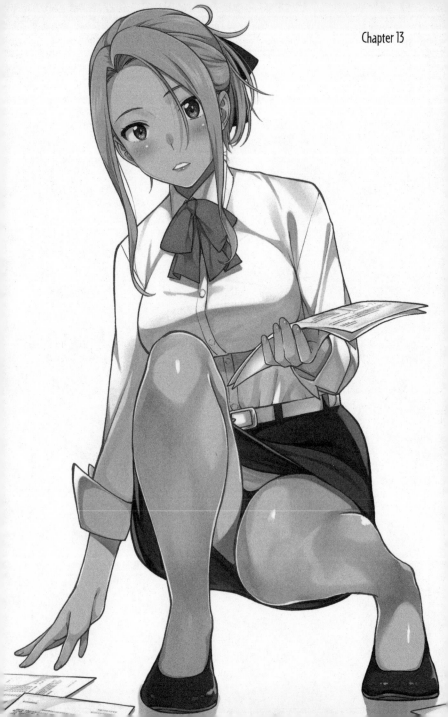

LUST GEASS

SOME TIME HAS PASSED SINCE YOU SUMMONED ME BY RECITING THAT SPELL...
AH... MM...
...BUT IT'S NOT YET TIME FOR US TO ENTER INTO A CONTRACT.
TAKA-TSUKI-KUN...
HUFF... HUFF...
CERTAINLY, YOU FEEL LUST FOR HIM.
HOWEVER, THAT CAN'T BE CALLED LOVE—NOT YET.
MM...

LET'S MEET AGAIN AFTER YOU CLEARLY FALL IN LOVE WITH HIM.
I'LL CREATE THE OPPORTUNITY.
YOU WEREN'T PART OF MY ORIGINAL PLAN, BUT THIS IS MORE ENJOYABLE WITH MANY PAWNS ON THE BOARD.
...WHAT IS IT? I FEEL LIKE I HAD ANOTHER STRANGE DREAM.
I BARELY REMEM-BER IT, BUT...
!
I'M WET AGAIN...
KUCHU (SQUISH)
WHAT'S WITH ME THESE DAYS?

... MAYBE IT'S THAT.
BECAUSE I SAW...
...TAKA-TSUKI-KUN AND USUI-SAN GOING AT IT...
SOMEHOW, THAT'S GOT ME ALL WORKED UP.
I'D BETTER GET MY HEAD BACK ON STRAIGHT.
HAAAH...
SHINO-SENSEIII!
SENSEI, THANKS FOR YOUR ADVICE THE OTHER DAY!
YUI TOOK YOUR ADVICE AND TOLD HIM HOW SHE FELT! NOW THEY'RE GOING OUT!
HEY... DON'T ANNOUNCE IT IN THE HALLWAY!

HEH-HEH. GOOD TO HEAR.
DATING IS FINE, BUT JUST BE SURE YOU DON'T LET IT GET IN THE WAY OF YOUR STUDYING.
YOU'RE AMAZING, SENSEI!
I GUESS YOUR WISDOM COMES FROM EXPERIENCE.
JUST HOW MANY BOYFRIENDS HAVE YOU HAD OVER THE YEARS?
NO COMMENT.
AH...

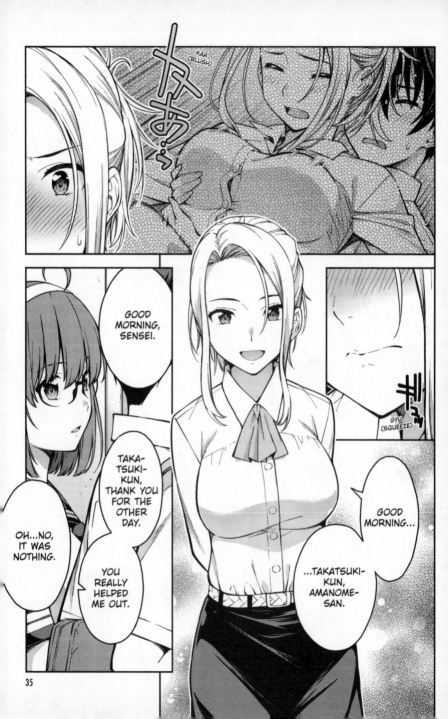

KAA (BLUSH)
GYU (SQUEEZE)
GOOD MORNING...
...TAKATSUKI-KUN, AMANOME-SAN.
GOOD MORNING, SENSEI.
TAKA-TSUKI-KUN, THANK YOU FOR THE OTHER DAY.
YOU REALLY HELPED ME OUT.
OH...NO, IT WAS NOTHING.

SOU-CHAN, DID SOMETHING HAPPEN WITH YOU AND SENSEI?
HE HELPED ME OUT AFTER SCHOOL LAST FRIDAY.
IT WAS VERY CHIVALROUS OF HIM.
AW, MAN...
I WISH I COULD'VE BEEN THERE TO SEE HIM BEING COOL.
IT REALLY WASN'T A BIG DEAL.
SENSEI IS EXAGGER-ATING.
I STILL WISH I COULD HAVE SEEN IT...
WELL, SENSEI, IF ANYTHING ELSE COMES UP, WE'LL BE COUNTING ON YOUR ADVICE!
SURE THING.
SEE? WASN'T SENSEI'S ADVICE RIGHT ON THE MONEY?
YEAH.
ADVICE FROM SOMEONE WITH A LOT OF ROMANTIC EXPERIENCE SURE IS VALUABLE.

A LOT...
YEAH, RIGHT ...
HON-ESTLY ...
...I KNOW I'M POPULAR.
SIGN: FACULTY ROOM
KIN (DING)
KON (DONG)
THAT'LL BE ALL FOR TODAY.
BE CAREFUL GOING HOME.
KAN (DANG)
KON
MANY STUDENTS HAVE CONFESSED THEIR LOVE TO ME...
...AS HAVE MY COL-LEAGUES.
TATEAKI-SENSEI.

I BROUGHT BACK LOCAL SWEETS AFTER VISITING MY PARENTS OVER THE WEEKEND. WANT SOME?
WE CAN HAVE THEM OVER TEA.
SORRY, I HAVE PLANS TODAY.
I'LL SEE YOU TOMORROW.
PON (PAT)
I TOLD YOU NOT TO BOTHER.
SHE'S JUST NOT INTO YOU.
SOB...
BUT... THIS ISN'T THE REAL ME.
17:01

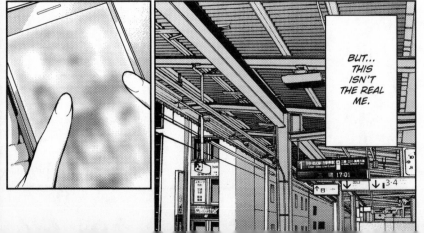

SHEESH... YOU'RE SUCH A KLUTZ, KOHAKU.
HERE.
JAINA-KUN...!
TOKUN (THUMP)
MY HEART...
...IS BEATING LIKE A JACK-HAMMER.

にへらぁ
NIHERAA (GRIN)
AWWWWWW...
JAINA-KUN IS SO CUTE...
ANY-WAY...
...I CAN'T BELIEVE MY ADVICE WORKED AGAIN.
"JUST HOW MANY BOYFRIENDS HAVE YOU HAD OVER THE YEARS?"
NOW THAT I'VE GOT THIS REPUTATION, I CAN'T TELL THEM THE TRUTH—IT'S ZERO!
I'VE JUST BEEN GIVING OUT ROMANTIC ADVICE BASED ON BITS AND PIECES OF MANGA I READ A LONG TIME AGO.
WHO WOULD'VE THOUGHT IT'D TURN OUT TO BE GOOD ADVICE?
BUT BECAUSE OF THAT, EVERYONE MISTAKENLY THINKS I'M SOME ROMANTIC GURU WITH A PLETHORA OF EXPERIENCE.

I LOVE YOU...
...KOHAKU.
JAINA-KUN...
IF I COULD HAVE...
...THIS KIND OF ROMANCE...
!!
THE NEW VOLUME CAME OUT YESTERDAY.
I HAVE TO GET IT!
THE PREMIUM BONUSES ARE...THIS AND THIS. I HAVE TO AT LEAST GET THESE TWO.

ZA (RUSTLE)
AHHHHHH...
THIS IS MORE LIKE IT.
THAT'S RIGHT. THIS IS MY TRUE SELF.
I'D BETTER GET A MOVE ON.
WHEN I'M AT SCHOOL, I'M JUST PLAYING A ROLE.
PA

HEE HEE HEE!
THAT'S ONE OF THE BONUS ILLUSTRATIONS DOWN! ♪
CITY
NOW ON TO THE NEXT BOOK-STORE...
IN FACT, MAYBE I'LL JUST GO ALL THE WAY TO SHINJUKU SO I'LL HAVE A COMPLETE SET OF THE BONUSES...
THAT WAS A GREAT CAFÉ...
... KATOU-SAN.

A FRIEND RECOMMENDED IT TO ME...
I'M GLAD YOU LIKED IT.
THAT'S THE GIRL I GAVE ADVICE TO.
EVEN THOUGH FINALS ARE COMING UP, SHE'S OUT GALLIVANTING.
DON'T BLAME ME IF YOUR GRADES FALL, GIRL.
EVEN THOUGH SHE ONLY HAS A BOYFRIEND THANKS TO ME, SHE BREEZES RIGHT BY WITHOUT REALIZING...
WELL ...
...IF SHE DID NOTICE, IT WOULD BE BAD.
THE PERSON I AM AT SCHOOL IS A FRAUD...
...BUT BECAUSE OF THAT, THE STUDENTS HAVE FAITH IN ME.
AN ABUNDANCE OF ROMANTIC EXPERIENCE
NORMIE
BEAUTIFUL
ZERO ROMANTIC EXPERIENCE
GEEK
PLAIN
I CAN'T LET THEM KNOW THAT THIS IS WHAT I'M REALLY LIKE.

...I COULD'VE HAD A ROMANCE LIKE THAT.

BUT I WISH...

I HAVE JAINA-KUN...

...AND THIS BONUS ILLUSTRATION IS CUTE TOO!

WHAT AM I THINKING ...!?

WAIT ...

NIYA (GRIN)

NIYA

BUN (SHAKE)

BUN

SORRY.

ARE YOU OKAY?

HIRA (FLUTTER)

WAH!

DON (BUMP)

EEEK!

45

T-TAKA-TSUKI-KUN!!?

SUTA
(TROT)

AH...

HE DIDN'T REALIZE IT WAS ME, DID HE...?

SUTA

IT'S OKAY.
HE DIDN'T NOTICE THAT TIME AT THE MOVIE THEATER...
...SO I SHOULD BE...
UM...
EXCUSE ME!
!!!
BIKI (TWITCH)
DON'T TELL ME... HE REALIZES!?
PU (SNICKER)
SENSEI... IT'S LIKE YOU'RE A TOTALLY DIFFERENT PERSON THAN AT SCHOOL.
DIDN'T I RUN INTO YOU LIKE THIS AT THE MOVIE THEATER?
SO YOU LIKE ANIME, HUH? AND YOU WERE ALONE THEN...I'M SURPRISED.
THIS IS BAD...

GEEZ...
WHY IS HE...
...CHASING AFTER ME!?
ZURU (SLIP)
BITAN (WHAM)

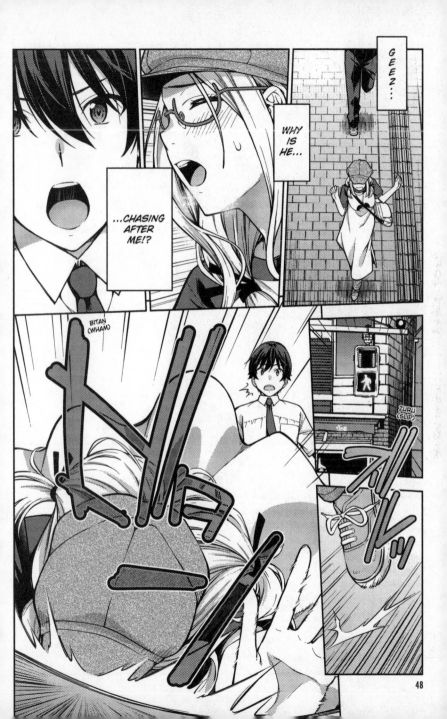

ARE YOU ALL RIGHT ...?
OWWW...
YOU ...
... DROPPED THIS.
EH...?
TH-THANK YOU.
HE CHASED ME DOWN TO RETURN THIS?
CHIKA (FLICKER) チカ
CHIKA チカ
AH... THE LIGHT'S CHANGING ALREADY.
CAN YOU STAND UP?
... AH.
THIS IS LIKE...

SHEESH...
YOU'RE SUCH A KLUTZ, SHINO.
I NEVER THOUGHT...

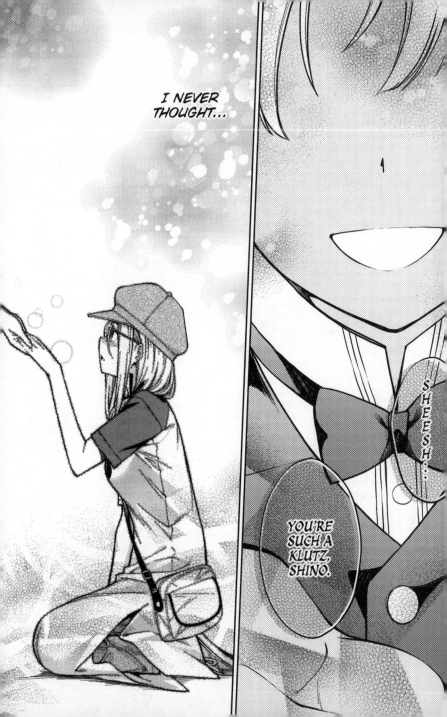

...THINGS LIKE THIS...
...ACTUALLY HAPPENED IN REALITY.
TOKUN (THUMP)

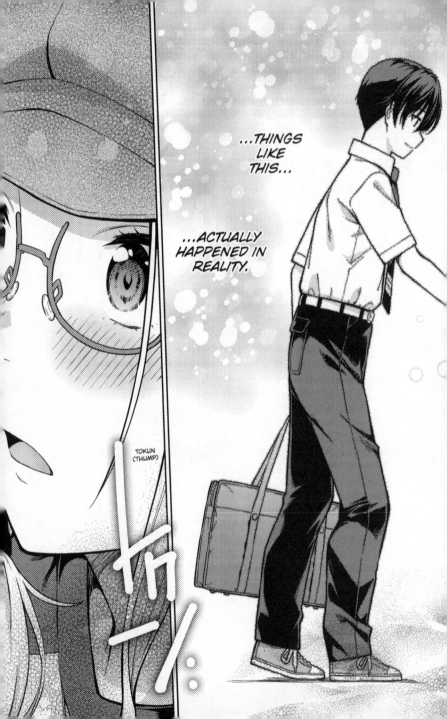

114 吉祥寺通り Kichijoji-dori Ave.
WELL, THEN—
PLEASE BE CAREFUL.
-dori Ave.
BOOO (DAZED)
360m
480m
AH...
OKAY...
TAKATSUKI-KUN... HE DOESN'T REALIZE IT'S ME?
AND YET, HE...
DOKI (BADUM)
DOKI
DOKI

MM...
TAKA-TSUKI... KUN...
NO...
WE CAN'T DO THIS, TAKATSUKI-KUN...
WE'RE...
...TEACHER AND STUDENT.

THAT'S WHAT YOU SAY, SENSEI...
...BUT YOUR BODY WANTS ME.
HUFF HUFF...
N-NO, IT DOESN'T.
HEH-HEH. IT LOOKS LIKE THE TIME IS RIPE.
KUCHU (SLURP)
KUCHU
I CAN TURN THE SIGHT YOU'RE SEEING NOW INTO REALITY.
IF YOU ENTER INTO A CONTRACT WITH ME, THAT IS...

CON... TRACT ...?
I CAN MAKE THAT DREAM COME TRUE.
HOWEVER, THAT WILL MAKE YOUR LUST JUST A BIT UNMAN-AGEABLE.
BUT THAT SHOULDN'T BE A PROBLEM.
YOU JUST NEED THE PERSON YOU LOVE TO HELP YOU QUELL YOUR DESIRE.
WELL? I'M NOT GOING TO COMPEL YOU TO DO ANYTHING.
JUST... IF YOU WISH TO HAVE A RELATIONSHIP WITH HIM, SAY THESE WORDS.
"ZEPAR, I AGREE TO ENTER INTO A CONTRACT WITH YOU."
... ZEPAR ...
I AGREE TO ENTER...
...INTO A... CON-TRACT ...
... WITH YOU.

I HAD ANOTHER WEIRD DREAM, DIDN'T I?

BUT I FEEL LIKE THIS ONE WAS A LITTLE BETTER THAN THE USUAL...

YAWN...

MM...

MORN-ING...

I THINK TAKATSUKI-KUN WAS IN IT...

...BUT I CAN'T REMEMBER WHAT IT WAS ABOUT.

KO (TAP)

WHAT'S THIS...?

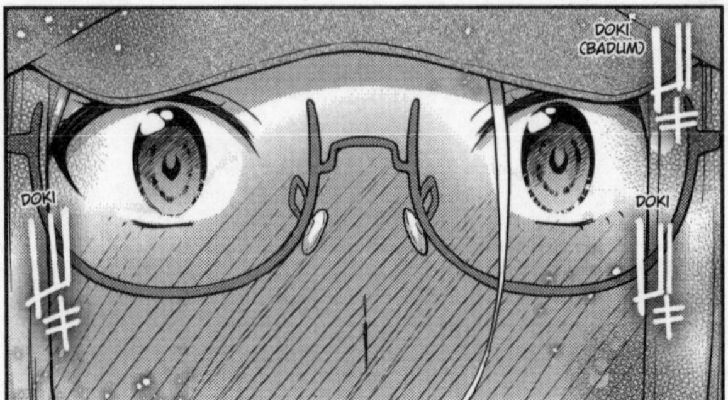
DOKI
(BADUM)
DOKI
DOKI

LUST GEASS

SOU-CHAN, MAKOTO-CHAN AND I WANNA STOP AT A BOOKSTORE ON THE WAY. IS THAT OKAY WITH YOU?

SURE THING.

Chapter 14

TAKA-TSUKI-KUN.

CAN I TALK TO YOU FOR A MINUTE?

SORRY. YOU TWO CAN GO ON AHEAD.

DID YOU DO SOMETHING, TAKATSUKI-KUN?

OKAY. JUST TEXT ME WHEN YOU'RE DONE.

NO, NOT AS FAR AS I KNOW...

WHAT DID YOU WANT TO TALK ABOUT, SENSEI?
AND WHY HERE?
GOOD QUES-TION...
I WASN'T SURE WHETHER I SHOULD BRING THIS UP...
THE OTHER DAY...
...WHAT WERE YOU AND USUI-SAN DOING IN HERE?
EH...?
WH-WHAT DID YOU JUST SAY...?

I DON'T MEAN TO MEDDLE IN STUDENTS' PRIVATE LIVES...
...BUT CONSIDERING THE LOCATION...
...I FINALLY THOUGHT IT WAS NECESSARY TO BRING IT UP.
W-WELL, THAT...
WAIT—SHE SAW US...?
BUT HOW CAN I EXPLAIN IT...?
TELLING HER IT WAS A DEMON'S CURSE WOULDN'T FLY.
WHAT'S WRONG?
YOU CAN'T ANSWER?
IT'S...
TAKATSUKI-KUN.
MAYBE IT HAD...

...SOME-THING...
...TO DO WITH THIS?
!!?
WHY DOES SENSEI HAVE A BOOK...!? SHE ALREADY RETURNED USUI'S COPY.
A THIRD COPY OF THE BOOK ...?
AND I RETURNED RIKKA'S COPY.

HOW DOES...
...SENSEI HAVE THAT!?
SENSEI... WHERE DID YOU GET THAT BOOK?
TAKA-TSUKI-KUN.
PIRA (FLAP)
WOULD YOU DO TO ME...
...WHAT YOU DID TO USUI-SAN THAT DAY?

W-WAIT A SECOND, SENSEI.
DO YOU KNOW WHAT YOU'RE SAYING...?
PURUN (JIGGLE)
YOU CAN'T DO IT?
EVEN THOUGH YOU DID IT WITH USUI-SAN...
...YOU WOULDN'T BE HAPPY WITH ME?
IT'S NO GOOD.
IF SHE'S THIS FAR GONE, SHE WON'T COME TO HER SENSES UNLESS WE DO IT ONCE.

BUT...
SENSEI, DON'T YOU HAVE A BOYFRIEND OR SOME-THING?
YOU SHOULD DO THAT KIND OF THING WITH THE PERSON YOU'RE DATING—
WHAT ABOUT YOU, TAKATSUKI-KUN? ARE YOU DATING USUI-SAN?
WHAT ABOUT AMANOME-SAN?
HUFF...
WELL, THAT...
AT THIS RATE, SENSEI AND I ARE GOING TO...
PIKU (TWITCH)
... SENSEI?

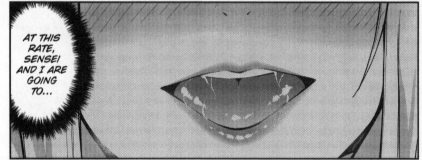

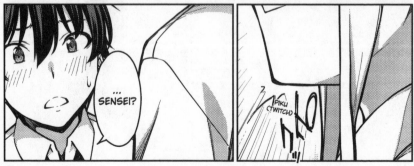

I'M SORRY.

YOU CAN GO...

I JUST CAN'T DO THIS...

I CAN'T...

WHY IS EVERY-THING GETTING BLURRY...?

HUH...?

AH... BUT...

SENSEI, IS YOUR BODY OKAY...?

FURA (WOBBLE)

DOSA (WHUMP)

SENSEI...!?

......
SOMEONE'S VOICE...?
THANK GOODNESS, SHINO.
YOU WOKE UP.
JAINA-KUN?
HOW DOES HE KNOW MY NAME...?
I WAS WORRIED ABOUT YOU.
YOU SUDDENLY COLLAPSED.
BUT I'M SO HAPPY.
JAINA-KUN LIKES ME—

HA (GASP)
!!?
THIS IS...
WAS I SLEEPING?
THEN JAINA-KUN WAS JUST A DREAM?
WHAT AM I THINKING? OF COURSE HE WAS!
JAINA-KUN IS JUST A MANGA CHARACTER.
HAAAAH...
I SAW MY WISH COME TRUE—A MANGA-LIKE ROMANCE.
...AH.
DID YOU WAKE UP?

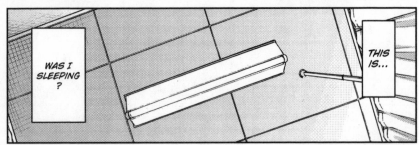

I WAS WORRIED. YOU SUDDENLY COL-LAPSED.
TAKA-TSUKI-KUN!?
WHAT'S HE DOING HERE...?
SEN-SEI...
HEY, SHINO.
GOOD MORN-ING.
AH... SENPAI.
TAKATSUKI BROUGHT YOU HERE.
ARE YOU ANE-MIC?

... THAT'S RIGHT.
I TOOK TAKATSUKI-KUN TO AN EMPTY CLASSROOM.
AND THEN ...
AND THEN ...
YOU'RE FLUSHED.
DO YOU HAVE A FEVER?
KAAA (BLUSH)
...WELL, YOU CAN HEAD HOME FOR TODAY.
YOU TOO, TAKATSUKI.
OH, AND ALSO, BE SURE TO THANK TAKATSUKI.
HE CARRIED YOU HERE AND WATCHED OVER YOU UNTIL YOU WOKE UP.
...
OH... IT'S NOTHING.
I WAS JUST WORRIED.

TAKA-TSUKI-KUN...
...RE-MINDS ME OF JAINA-KUN.
...THANK YOU...
...TAKA-TSUKI-KUN.
IT'S GOTTEN PRETTY LATE.
...SO, SENSEI ...
...DO YOU FEEL ALL RIGHT?
TAKA-TSUKI-KUN...
...HELPED ME OUT AGAIN TODAY.

DOKI
(BADUM)

DOKI

I―...?

UM...

ABOUT
THAT
BOOK...

WHY
IS
IT...

...WHEN
I'M
WITH
TAKA-
TSUKI-
KUN...

...

SEN-
SEI...?

NO.

I
CAN'T.

GYU
(SQUEEZE)

I
CAN'T
...

...LET
MYSELF
FEEL
THIS
WAY.

TAKATSUKI-
KUN IS MY
STUDENT
AND MUCH
YOUNGER
THAN ME...

BUT ...
TOKUN (THUMP)
...EVEN THOUGH I KNOW IT'S WRONG...
...I STILL...

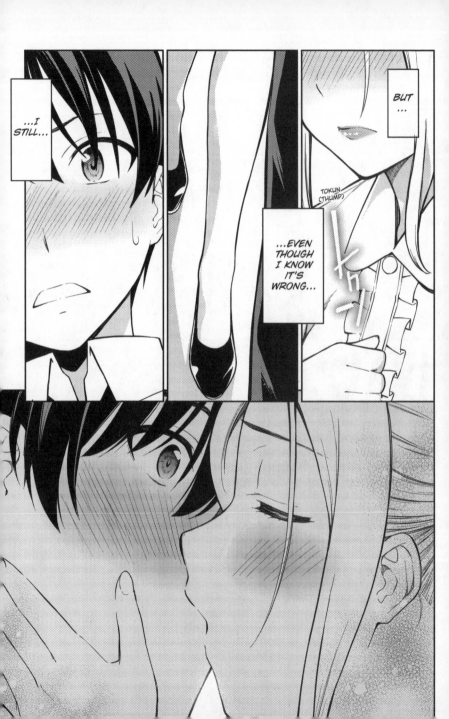

MM...
KUCHU (SMACK)
KUCHU
S...
SENSEI ...!!
BA (SWISH)
YOU REALLY ARE...
TAKA-TSUKI-KUN, I HAVE A FAVOR TO ASK.
WOULD YOU...
...COME WITH ME?
...

LUST†GEASS

Chapter 15

I'M GOING WITH HER, LIKE SHE ASKED...

...BUT SHOULD I?

AT THIS RATE, I'M GOING TO END UP HAVING SEX WITH MY TEACHER.

HOW DID SHE GET THAT BOOK...?

I HAVE TO AT LEAST FIND THAT OUT FROM HER.

SENSEI, WOULD YOU TELL ME ALREADY?

WHERE DID YOU GET THAT BOOK?

...YOU WANT TO KNOW THAT BADLY?

THIS IS THE SAME PATTERN I HAD WITH USUI.

"IF YOU WANT TO KNOW, THEN DO IT WITH ME."

BUT SENSEI MUST HAVE A BOYFRIEND... RIGHT? I MEAN, SHE'S BEAUTIFUL.

SO... MAYBE, IF I DID IT WITH HER, IT WOULD JUST BE THIS ONCE.

I GUESS JUST ONCE WOULD BE—

GU (CLENCH)

HUFF! HUFF! HUFF!

I APOLOGIZE, TAKATSUKI-KUN. SORRY, BUT PLEASE GO HOME.

N-NO. I...

I CAN'T DO THIS AFTER ALL...

BASA (FWAP)

AH!

AH... I'LL GET IT.

I DROPPED IT. I'M SO CLUMSY...

FURA (WOBBLE)

EH...? BUT—

GOSO (RUMMAGE)

GOSO

IF YOU NEED THE BOOK, I'LL GIVE IT TO YOU NOW, BUT PLEASE...

TOSA (WHUMP)
S-SENSEI!?
!!
SENSEI, YOU HAVE A FEVER...
IT'S OKAY... I'LL BE FINE.
HUFF...
HUFF...

NO, YOU'RE OBVIOUSLY NOT FINE. I'LL TAKE YOU HOME.
TAKATSUKI-KUN'S SCENT...
WHY DOES IT MAKE...
...MY HEART BEAT SO FAST?
TON (SHOVE)
THANK YOU FOR WALKING ME THIS FAR.
SEE YOU TOMOR-ROW.
AH...
SENSEI ...
...

THIS IS MY APARTMENT.

YOU CAN GO NOW. IF ANYONE FOUND OUT THAT I BROUGHT A STUDENT INTO MY APARTMENT, I'D BE FIRED.

R-RIGHT.

BOOO (DAZED)

BUT WILL YOU REALLY BE ALL RIGHT? DO YOU HAVE MEDICINE?

MEDI-CINE...?

WHAT KIND?

I'LL GO BUY SOME, THEN. YOU WAIT HERE.
OKAY, I GUESS...
THANK YOU.
YOU REALLY ARE KIND, TAKATSUKI-KUN.
YOU'RE LIKE JAINA-KUN.
JAINA ...?
ANYWAY, I'LL BE RIGHT BACK.
AH...
THIS IS WHERE...

ANYWAY, I'LL BE RIGHT BACK, KOHAKU.
AH...
JAINA-KUN.
WAIT...
DON'T GO...!!

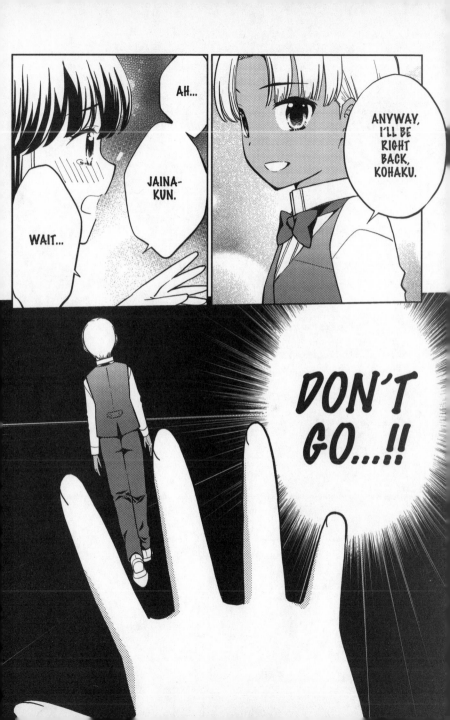

IT'S LIKE THAT SCENE WITH KOHAKU AND JAINA-KUN, RIGHT BEFORE THEY'RE SEPARATED...
AT THAT TIME, JAINA-KUN SAID...
...HE'D BE RIGHT BACK, BUT—
DON'T GO...
JIWA (TRICKLE)
DON'T ...
DON'T LEAVE ME ALONE...

—INO.
MM...
HEY, SHINO.
COME ON, WAKE UP.
ARE YOU OKAY?
URU (WATER)
URU
AH...
JAINA-KUN.
THANK GOD! YOU CAME BACK TO ME...!!
GYUU (SQUEEZE)
WHA...!? W-WAIT A SECOND...!

CALM DOWN, SENSEI.
WHAT'S THIS ABOUT "JAINA-KUN"?
EH...?
TAKATSUKI-KUN? WHAT ARE YOU DOING HERE...?
...I BOUGHT YOU MEDICINE.
ANYWAY, SENSEI, LET GO OF ME.
IF SOMEBODY SAW US HERE LIKE THIS—
MM...
KUCHU (SLURP)
KUCHU

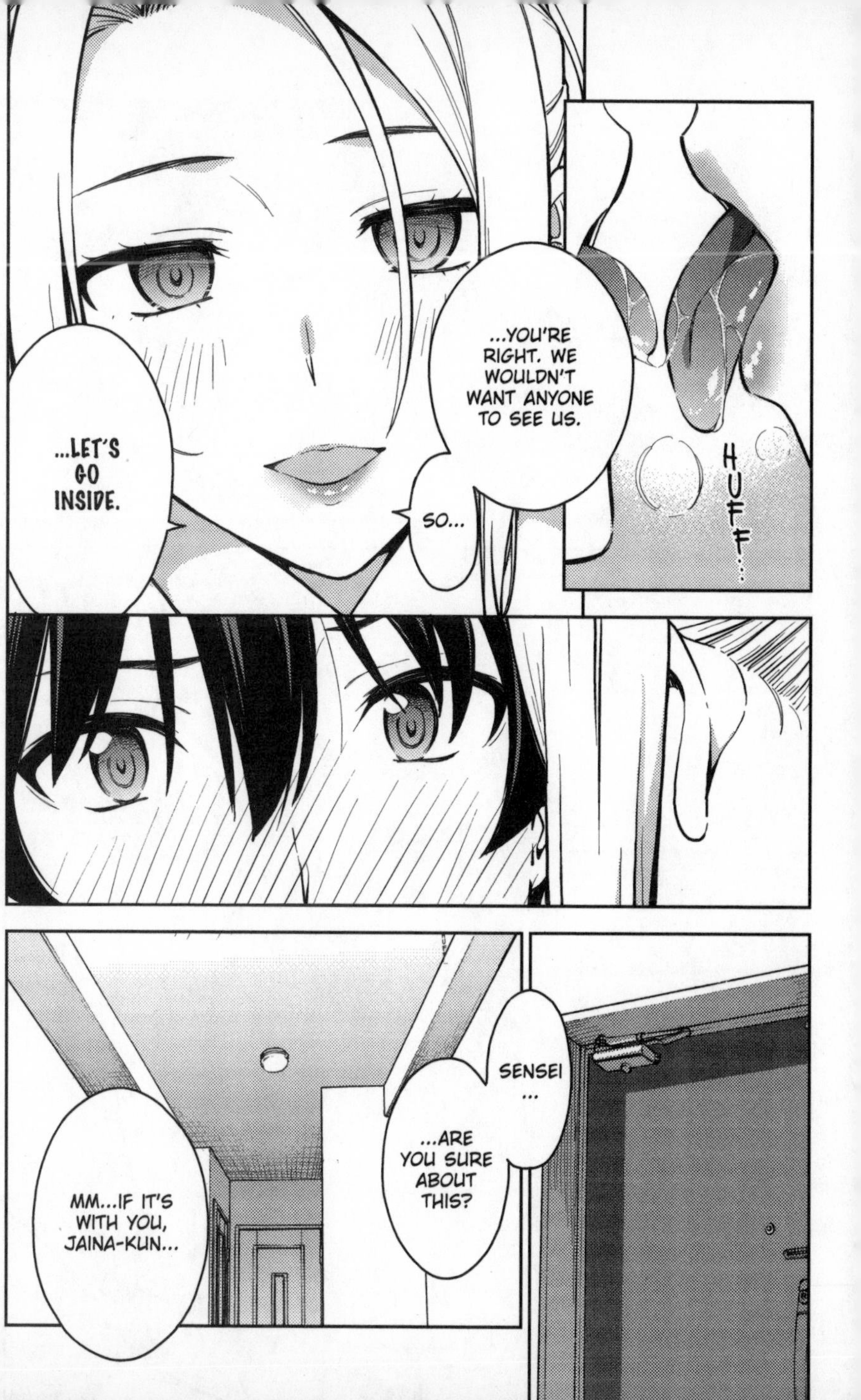
HUFF...
...YOU'RE RIGHT. WE WOULDN'T WANT ANYONE TO SEE US.
SO...
...LET'S GO INSIDE.
SENSEI...
...ARE YOU SURE ABOUT THIS?
MM...IF IT'S WITH YOU, JAINA-KUN...

UH, NO... I'M TAKATSUKI.
EH...?
I'M FINE EITHER WAY.
AH...
PIKUN (TWITCH)
SENSEI?
THIS IS MY FIRST TIME...
YOUR FIRST TIME...?

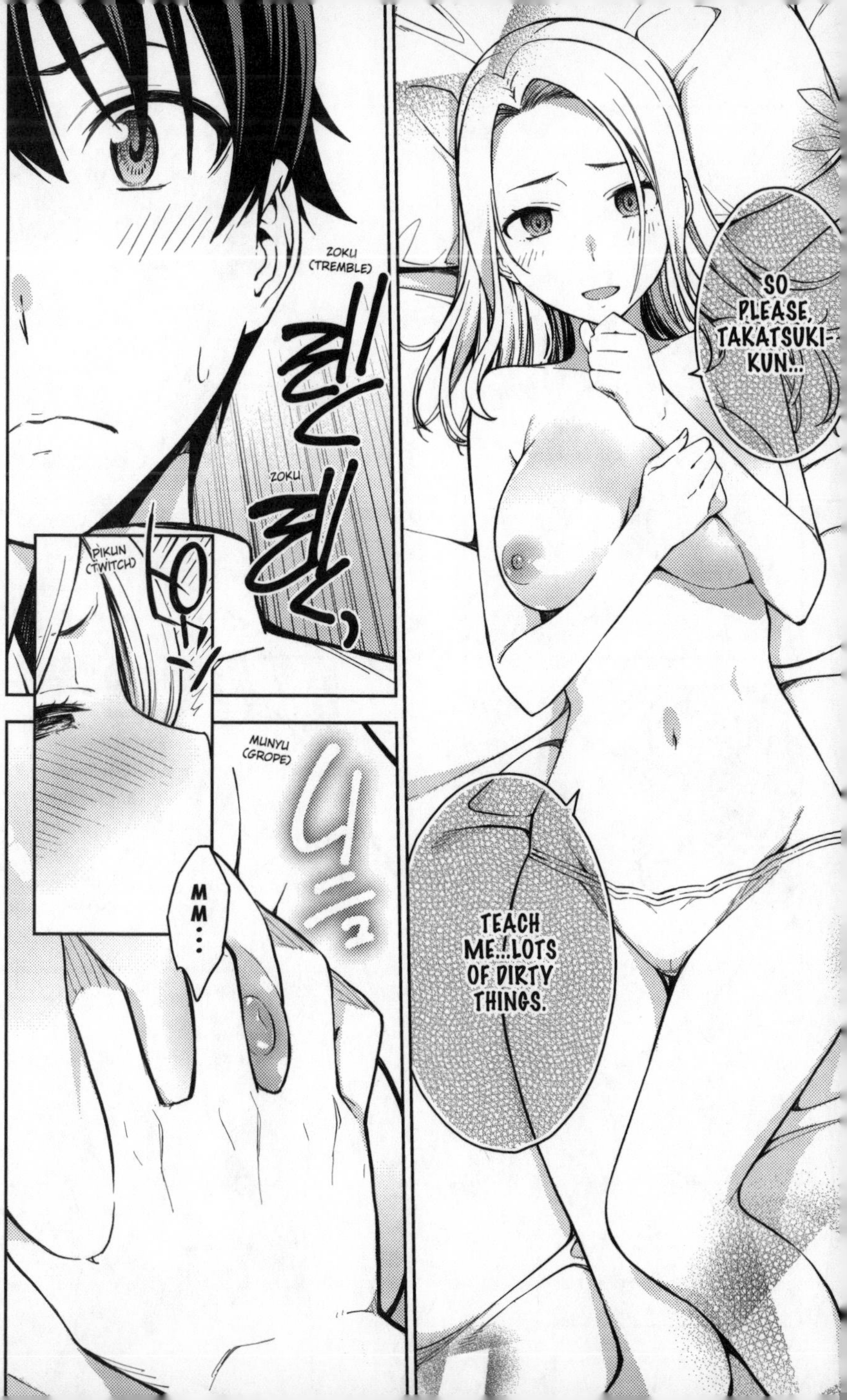
SO PLEASE, TAKATSUKI-KUN...
TEACH ME...LOTS OF DIRTY THINGS.
ZOKU (TREMBLE)
ZOKU
PIKUN (TWITCH)
MUNYU (GROPE)
MM...

AH... WHAT IS THIS? AMAZING!
HUFF!
HUFF...
WOW...
HUFF...
IT FEELS ...
...SO GOOD.
HUFF...♥
PERO (CLICK)
AHHH...
OHHH... TAKATSUKI-KUN, DON'T SUCK ON THEM.
AH!
KUCHU (SLURP)
CHUU (SUCK)
HUFF!
YOU'RE... DRIVING ME CRAZY...

SENSEI... YOU NEED TO LOOSEN UP.

WOULD YOU... OPEN YOUR LEGS?

EH...?

...AH.

GOSO (RUSTLE)

YOUR NAME...

DON'T CALL ME "SENSEI." IT SOUNDS TOO...FORMAL FOR THIS.

CALL ME BY MY NAME.

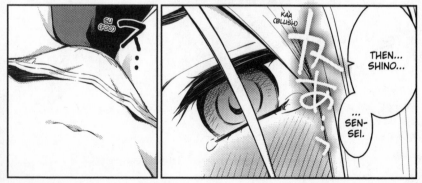

SU (FOO)

KAA (BLUSH)

THEN... SHINO...

...SEN-SEI.

KUCHU (SQUISH)
!!?
ZOKU (SHUDDER)
WHA... WHAT IS THIS...?
ZOKU
WAIT...
I CAN'T HANDLE THIS...
SHINO-SENSEI ...!
BURU (QUIVER)
BURU

BIKUN
(TWITCH)
AAAAAH—♡

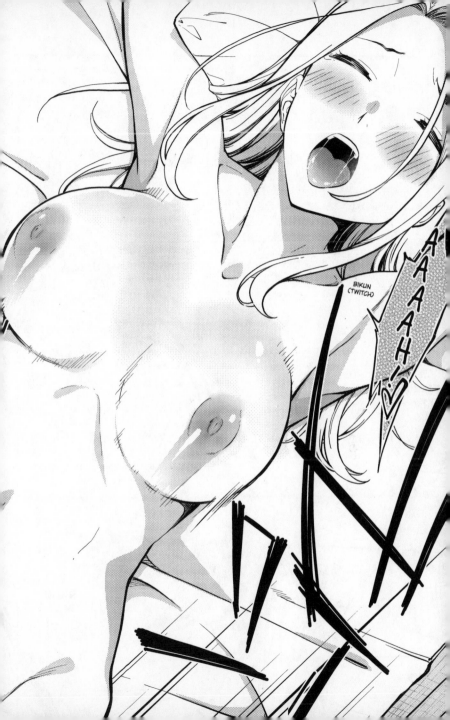

AH...AAAAH!♡
BIKUN
HUFF...
HUFF...♥

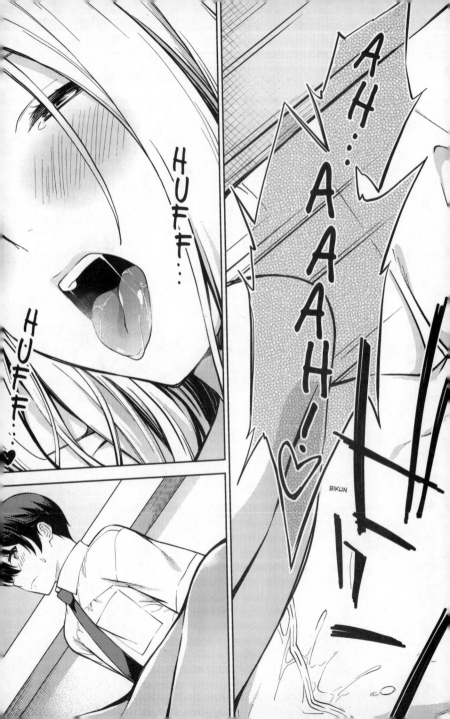

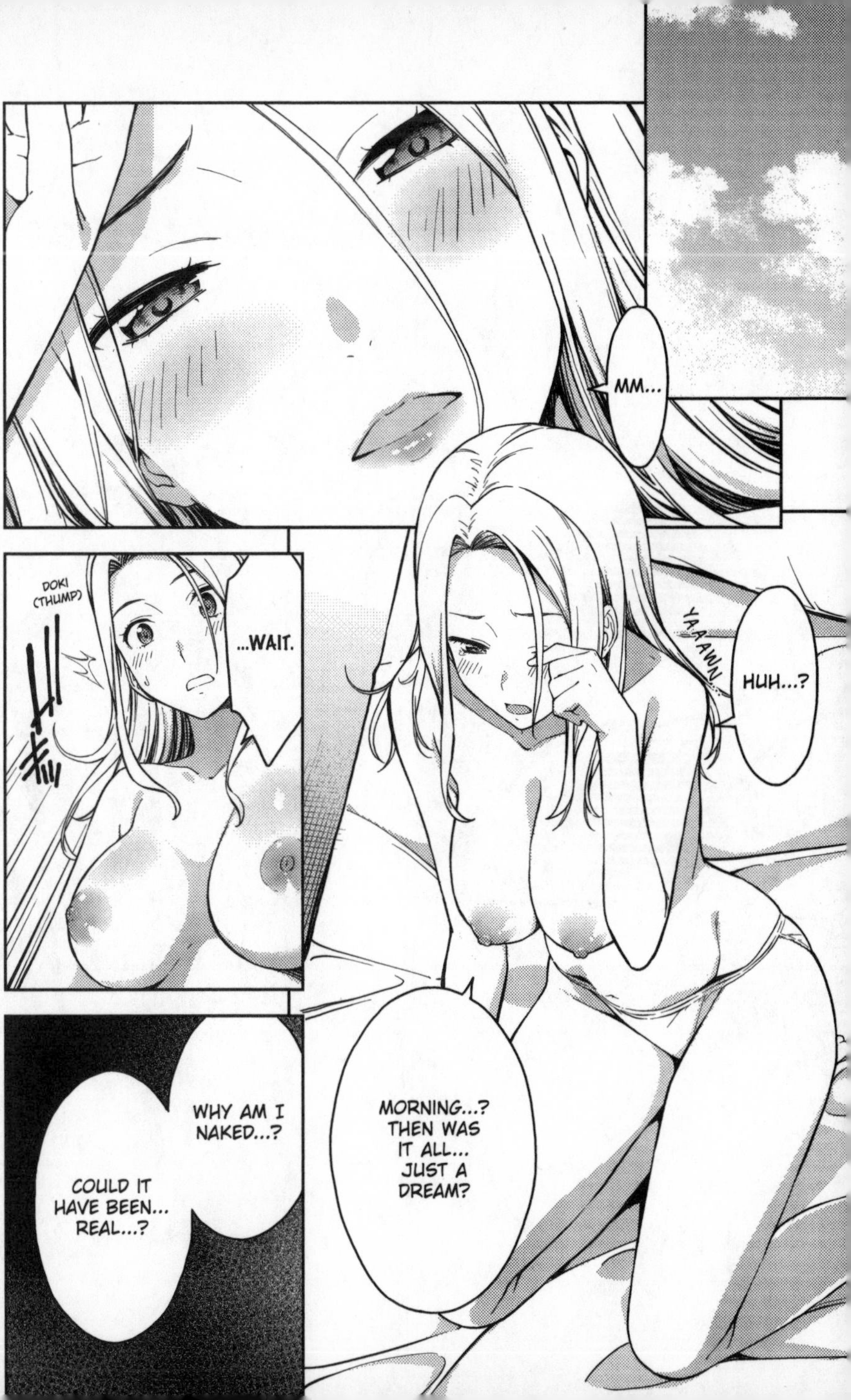
MM...
YAAAWN
HUH...?
MORNING...? THEN WAS IT ALL... JUST A DREAM?
DOKI (THUMP)
...WAIT.
WHY AM I NAKED...?
COULD IT HAVE BEEN... REAL...?

JIWA
(TRICKLE)
じわ

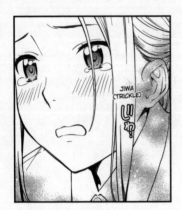

Chapter 16
I NEVER THOUGHT I WOULD DO THOSE THINGS WITH SENSEI.
WAS IT THE RIGHT THING TO DO?
BUT ONCE SOMEONE IS IN THAT STATE, THERE'S NO OTHER CHOICE...

ZEPAR... SHE EVEN PUT A CURSE ON SENSEI.
IT'S LIKE SHE'S MANIPU-LATING ALL OF US.
COME TO THINK OF IT...
...SENSEI WAS CALLING ME BY SOME WEIRD NAME.
"JAINA-KUN..." I FEEL LIKE I'VE HEARD THAT BEFORE SOMEWHERE...
PURU (BZZZ)
RURU
RU
Sou-chan, where are you?
Your dinner's getting cold!
RIKKA-CHAN, SORRY.
I'M ALMOST THERE.
OH, RIGHT. RIKKA, THERE'S SOMETHING I WANNA ASK YOU.
OUT OF ALL THE MANGA YOU OWN—

GOOD MORNING.

SHINO-SENSEI, GOOD MORNING!

WHAT'S WRONG, SENSEI?

...HUH?

BOOO (DAZED)

EH ...?

AH... GOOD MORNING.

COME ON, SENSEI, WHAT IS IT?

I'VE JUST GOT SOMETHING ON MY MIND...

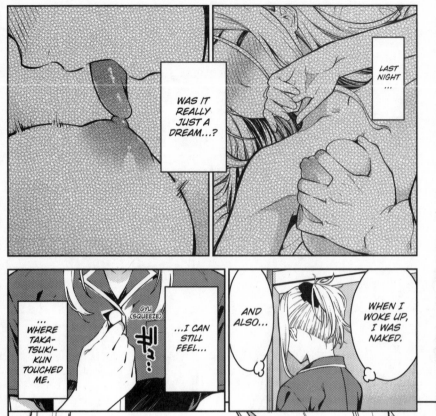

LAST NIGHT...
WAS IT REALLY JUST A DREAM...?
WHEN I WOKE UP, I WAS NAKED.
AND ALSO...
...I CAN STILL FEEL...
GYU (SQUEEZE)
... WHERE TAKA-TSUKI-KUN TOUCHED ME.
KAAA (BLUSH)

BUN (SHAKE)
BUN
GEEZ... WHAT AM I THINKING!?
THERE'S NO WAY THAT ACTUALLY HAPPENED!
IT'S IMPOS-SIBLE...!!

TAKA-TSUKI-KUN IS TAKING A NAP...
IS MY CLASS THAT BORING...?
HE INVADES MY DREAMS TO DO THAT TO ME...
KA (TAK)
jugem
WHY AM I THE ONLY ONE WHO HAS TO SUFFER FOR IT...?
TAKA-TSUKI-KUN!!
GABA (SWISH)
Y-YES !?
READ FROM THE TOP...
...OF PAGE FORTY-TWO.
...

UM...
HE COULD STAND TO BE A LITTLE MORE CONCERNED ABOUT ME.
New Morning
TAKATSUKI-KUN, READ THE NEXT PART.
EH...? ME AGAIN?
TAKA-TSUKI-KUN...!
AFTER SCHOOL
HUH?
YOU HAVE SOMETHING TO DO TODAY TOO?

EH...?

CH-CHEATING...?

EH!?

DON'T TELL ME YOU'RE CHEATING.

GIKU (GULP)

SORRY...

IT'S OKAY... BUT IT SEEMS YOU'VE BEEN BUSIER LATELY.

YEAH... I KNOW YOU WOULDN'T DO THAT, SOU-CHAN...

N-NO WAY—I'D NEVER!

SENSEI... IF SHE'S UNDER THE SAME CURSE AS RIKKA AND USUI...

...SHE'LL PROBABLY HAVE ANOTHER FIT OF UNCONTROL-LABLE LUST SOON UNLESS SHE SWALLOWS SEMEN.

THEN LET'S GO HOME TOGETHER, RIKKA.

OKAY. SEE YOU LATER, SOU-CHAN.

106

SHE FELL ASLEEP BEFORE WE GOT THAT FAR YESTERDAY...
...SO MY GUESS IS, RIGHT ABOUT NOW—
I WONDER WHERE SHE IS.
MAYBE SHE WASN'T FEELING WELL AGAIN...
保健室
GARA (RATTLE)
EX-CUSE ME.
IS TATEAKI-SENSEI HERE?
...HUH?
NO ONE'S HERE...?
...
MM...

SIGN: NURSE'S OFFICE

HUFF...
MM...
N-NO ...
I'M... MAKING NOISE...
KUCHU (RUB)
AH...
GUCHA (STROKE)
NUCHA (SQUISH)
HUFF!
AL-MOST...
HUFF...
...THERE...

EX-CUSE ME...
TATEAKI-SENSEI?
DOKI (BADUM)
WH-WHA...?
WHO IS IT...?
ASE (FRET)
AH...IT'S TAKATSUKI.
ARE YOU FEELING ILL AGAIN?
ASE
TAKA-TSUKI-KUN.
SHAAA (FWISH)
NOT ESPE-CIALLY...
I'M TIRED, SO I JUST CAME HERE TO REST FOR A BIT.
DOKI
DOKI
I HOPE HE DIDN'T HEAR ME MOANING...

SENSEI... ARE YOU SURE YOU FEEL ALL RIGHT...?

WHEN I STOPPED BY, SENPAI TOLD ME TO HOLD THE FORT AND LEFT...

...AND WHILE WAITING FOR HER TO COME BACK, I GOT SLEEPY.

I'M FINE.

HE DIDN'T NOTICE...? BUT...

I'M SURE SHE'S IN THE GYM. SENPAI USED TO PLAY BASKETBALL...

...AND EVEN NOW, SHE SHOOTS HOOPS THERE ONCE IN A WHILE.

...WHEN I THINK THAT I'M ALONE WITH TAKATSUKI-KUN...

GYU (SQUEEZE)

...MY HEART STARTS BEATING FAST.

OH REALLY...?

SO WHAT DID YOU COME HERE FOR, TAKA-TSUKI-KUN?
THIS IS THE NURSE'S OFFICE, BUT YOU DON'T SEEM UNWELL.
ACTU-ALLY...
...I WAS WORRIED ABOUT YOU...
...AND SUS-PECTED YOU MIGHT BE HERE.
EH ...?
DOKI (BADUM)
WH-WHAT DO YOU MEAN?
THERE'S NO REASON FOR YOU TO WORRY ABOUT ME.
BUT YESTER-DAY...
TAKA-TSUKI-KUN WORRIES ABOUT ME...
MORE IMPOR-TANTLY, WHAT WAS THAT IN TODAY'S CLASS?
BRAZENLY TAKING A NAP LIKE THAT...

OH, THAT ...
YOU'VE GOT FINALS NEXT WEEK.
DON'T BLAME ME IF YOU FLUNK.
...
I'M... GOING TO GO LOOK FOR SENPAI, SO...
...YOU GET ON HOME!
ALL I DID WAS LOOK HIM IN THE EYE...
WHY DO I FEEL LIKE THIS?
TA (TAP)
GOOD-BYE...!
AH...

"WAIT, KOHAKU.
"I'LL NEVER LEAVE YOU AGAIN."
JAINA-KUN ...?
FROM SHANGRI-LA WITH LOVE.
THE DIALOGUE FROM THE CLIMAX OF VOLUME 12.
HOW DID YOU KNOW THAT...?
WHEN YOU KEPT SAYING "JAINA-KUN" YESTERDAY, SENSEI, IT RANG A BELL.
I ASKED RIKKA IF THERE WAS A MANGA SERIES WITH A CHARACTER BY THAT NAME, AND SHE POINTED TO THIS.

SO I BORROWED THE SERIES FROM HER...
...AND STAYED UP ALL NIGHT READING IT.
THEN HE WAS NAPPING BEFORE BECAUSE—
WHY DID YOU GO TO ALL THE TROUBLE...?
BE-CAUSE...
...I WANTED TO KNOW MORE ABOUT YOU, SENSEI.
KAAA (BLUSH)
かぁぁ…っ

WH-WHY WOULD YOU WANT TO KNOW ABOUT ME?
SO YOU COULD LAUGH AT ME FOR READING MANGA?
EH?
WHY WOULD I?
AFTER ALL...
...DON'T YOU THINK IT'S CHILDISH, AT MY AGE?
I DON'T THINK THAT.
RIKKA HAS HUNDREDS OF VOLUMES HERSELF.
HMPH!
OH? YOU OBVIOUSLY KNOW A LOT ABOUT AMANOME-SAN.
OF COURSE YOU WOULD BE CLOSE.
I SUPPOSE YOU ARE CHILDHOOD FRIENDS.
UM, SENSEI... WHAT'S THE MATTER?

IT SEEMS YOU'RE CLOSE TO USUI-SAN TOO.
YOU'RE REALLY POPULAR, AREN'T YOU?
SO ARE YOU...
WORD IS YOU HAVE TONS OF ROMANTIC EXPERI-ENCE.
THAT'S...
...NONE OF YOUR BUSINESS.
... WAIT.
AH!
HUH?
H-H-HOW DO YOU KNOW ABOUT JAINA-KUN!?
HOW DID YOU KNOW HE WAS A MANGA CHARAC-TER...?
EH...? WELL, THERE WAS A LOT OF MANGA IN YOUR APARTMENT, SENSEI.

THEN YOU REALLY DID COME TO MY APARTMENT YESTERDAY, TAKATSUKI-KUN...?
YOU DON'T REMEMBER?
IT WASN'T A DREAM...?
TAKA-TSUKI-KUN...
...AND I REALLY DID...
PIKU (TWITCH)
GAKUN (WHUD)

WH- WHAT SHOULD I DO?
MY BODY IS HOT...
IT'S LIKE I HAVE AN ITCH THAT I CAN'T SCRATCH...
KUCHU (SQUISH)
NO... DON'T LOOK, TAKATSUKI-KUN.
MOMI (RUB)
MUNYU (GROPE)
I CAN'T CONTAIN MYSELF...
SENSEI... THAT MUST BE ZEPAR'S CURSE.
...ZEPAR? A CURSE?
I DON'T KNOW ABOUT ANY OF THAT...
THERE IS ONE WAY...
...TO CONTAIN IT.

TELL ME... IT'S LIKE... I'M NOT MYSELF.
ALL I CAN THINK ABOUT ARE DIRTY THINGS...
I...WOULD DO ANYTHING...
...TO GO BACK TO NORMAL.
TAKA-TSUKI-KUN.
WHAT AM I SUPPOSED TO DO?
UM...
YOU DON'T HAVE TO DO ANYTHING. JUST SIT STILL...

HUFF! HUFF! ♥
AH... MM...
MUNYU (GROPE)
むにゅ
MOMI (RUB)
もみ
...NO.
DON'T RUB THEM...
KYU (TWEAK)
AH! ♥
SENSEI, TRY TO RELAX MORE.
HUFF...
NO...
I'D SAY YOU'RE REALLY CUTE.
EASY FOR YOU TO SAY...
TAKATSUKI-KUN... DO YOU THINK I'M STRANGE?
COME ON... DON'T MOCK YOUR ELDERS.

KUCHU (SQUISH)
AH...
THAT'S...
NO...
HUFF!
TH...
THAT'S EMBARRASSING...
HUFF...
T-TAKATSUKI-KUN...!
BIKUN (TWITCH)
HUFF...

!!!?

ACTU-ALLY...

DOKI (BADUM)

KUTAA (DROOP)

AH... RIGHT. THIS ALONE ISN'T ENOUGH TO QUELL A FIT OF LUST.

TAKATSUKI-KUN...IT'S NOT GETTING BETTER YET.

YOU MEAN...

KAA (BLUSH)

DOKI

DOKI

TAKATSUKI-KUN, I REALLY HAVE TO DO THAT...?

DRINKING...

YES. THAT'S THE ONLY METHOD I KNOW.

...YOUR SEMEN...

122

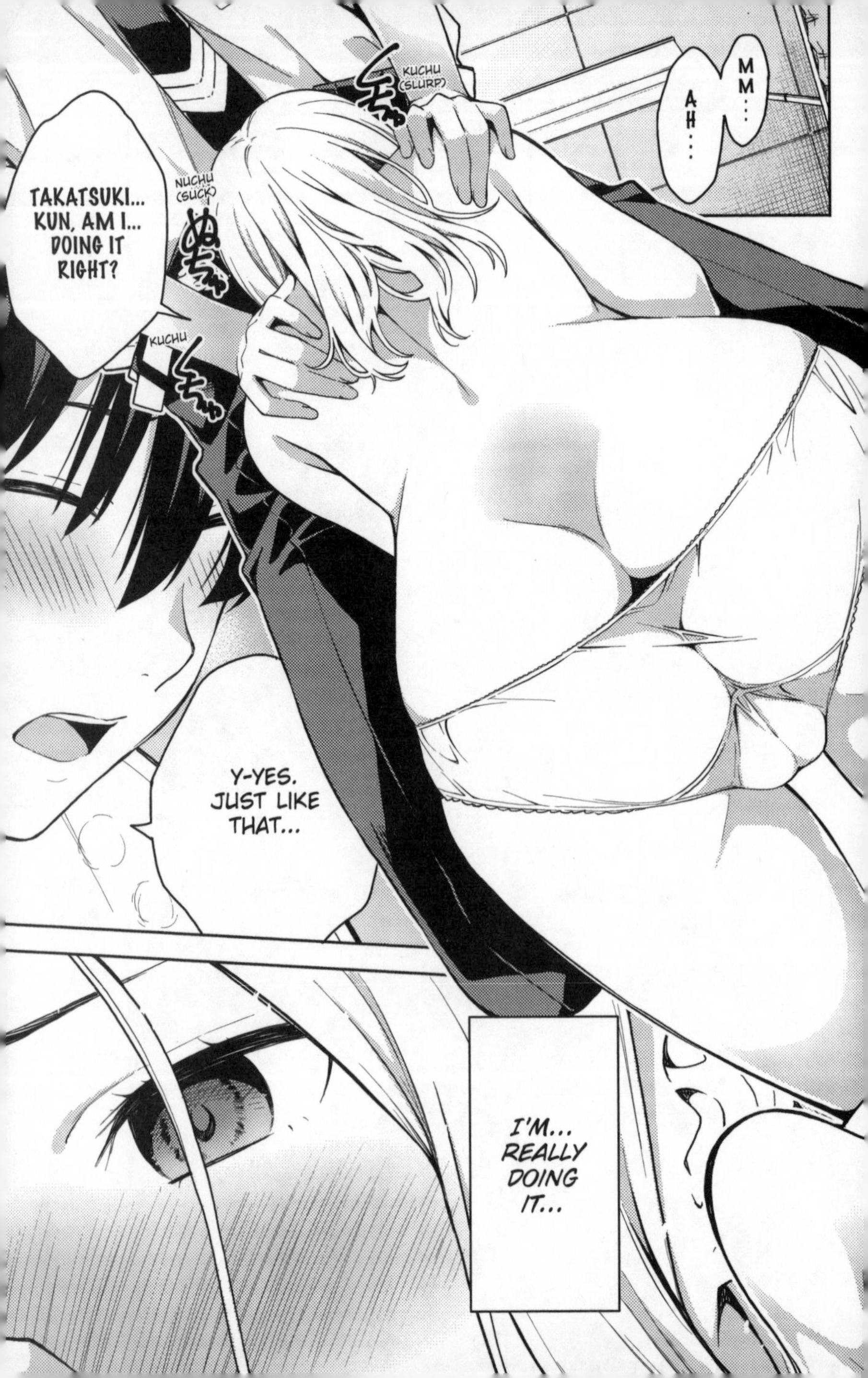
MM... AH...
KUCHU (SLURP)
NUCHU (SUCK)
KUCHU
TAKATSUKI... KUN, AM I... DOING IT RIGHT?
Y-YES. JUST LIKE THAT...
I'M... REALLY DOING IT...

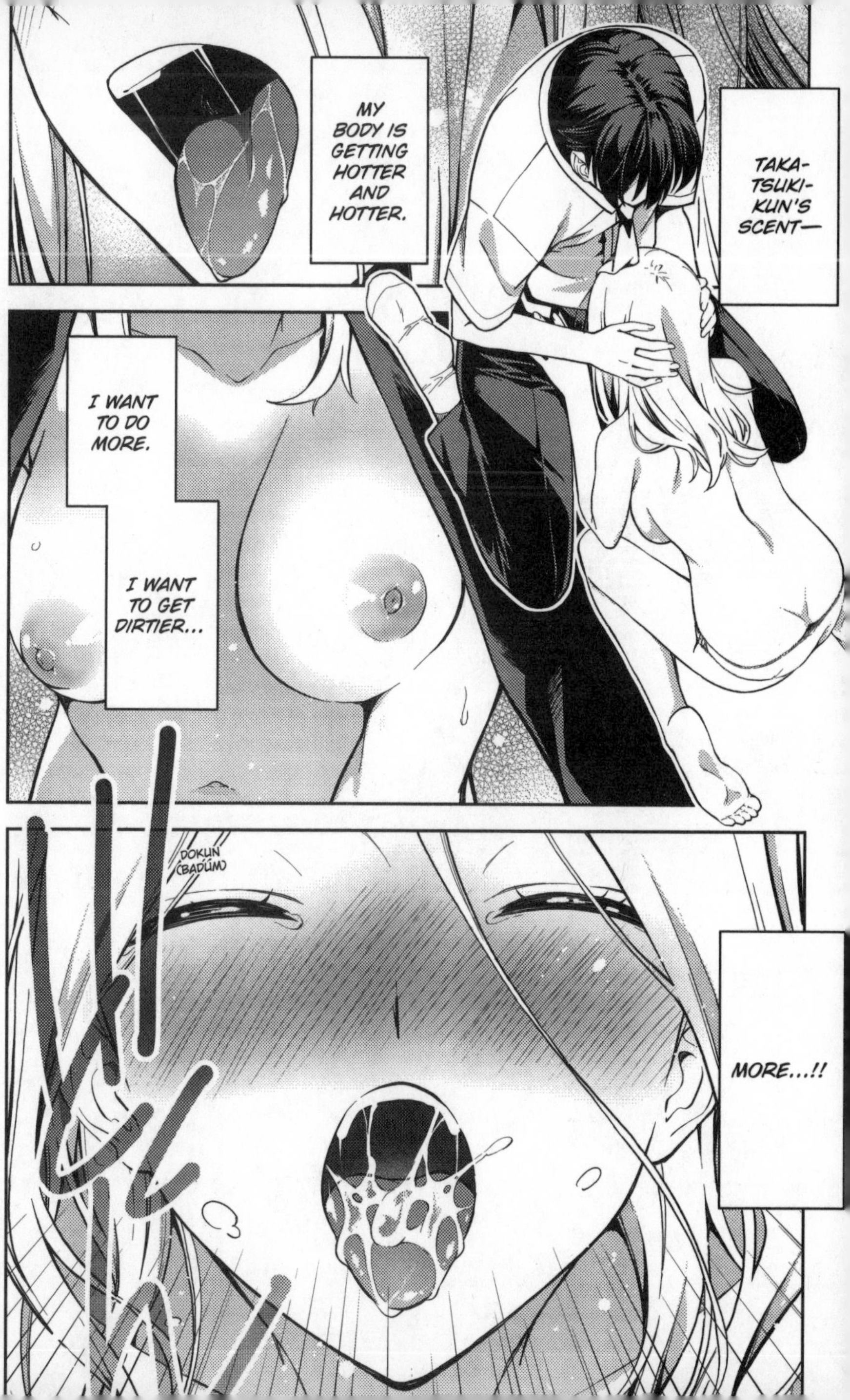
TAKA-TSUKI-KUN'S SCENT—
MY BODY IS GETTING HOTTER AND HOTTER.
I WANT TO DO MORE.
I WANT TO GET DIRTIER...
DOKUN (BADÚM)
MORE...!!

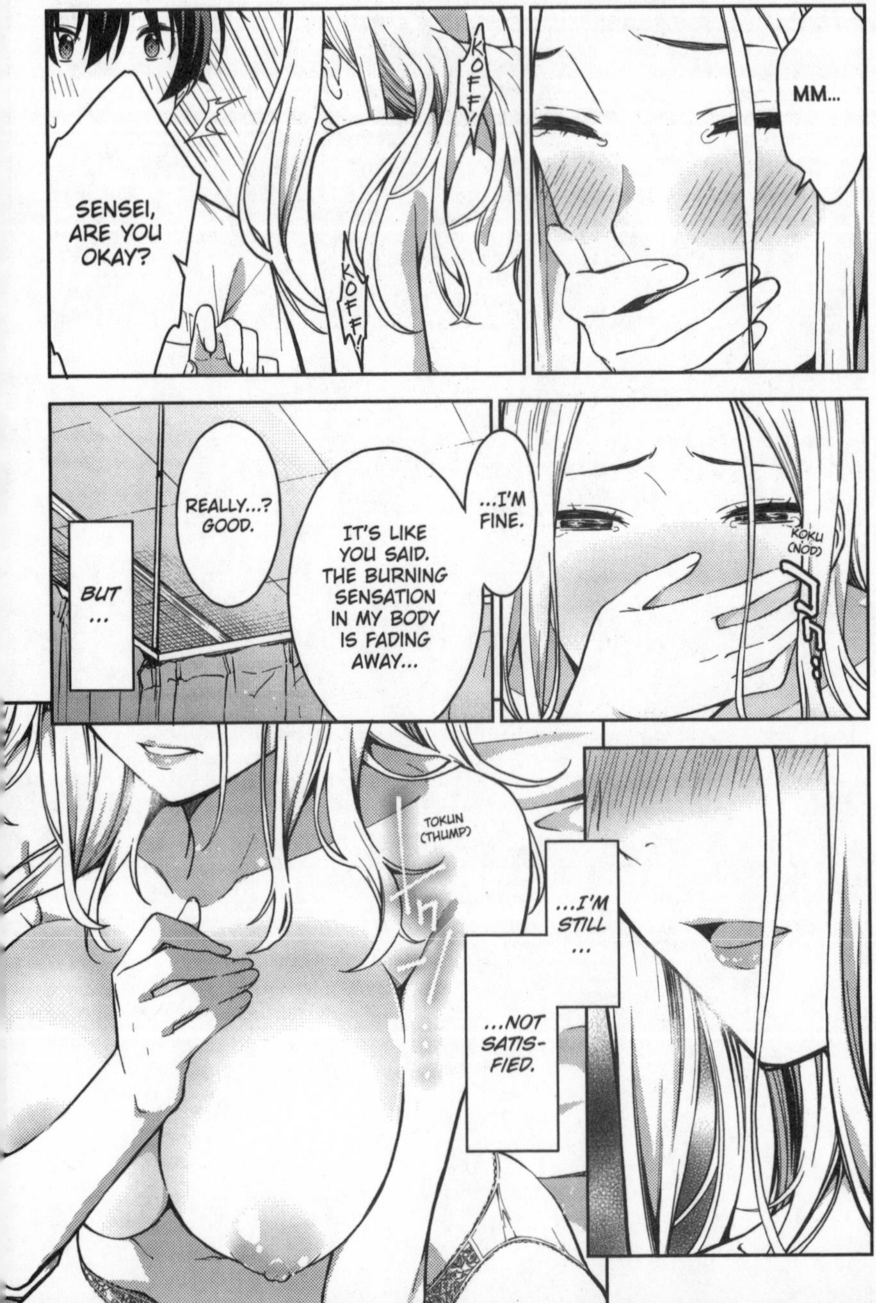
MM...
KOFF!
KOFF!
SENSEI, ARE YOU OKAY?
...I'M FINE.
KOKU (NOD)
IT'S LIKE YOU SAID. THE BURNING SENSATION IN MY BODY IS FADING AWAY...
REALLY...? GOOD.
BUT ...
...I'M STILL ...
...NOT SATIS-FIED.
TOKUN (THUMP)

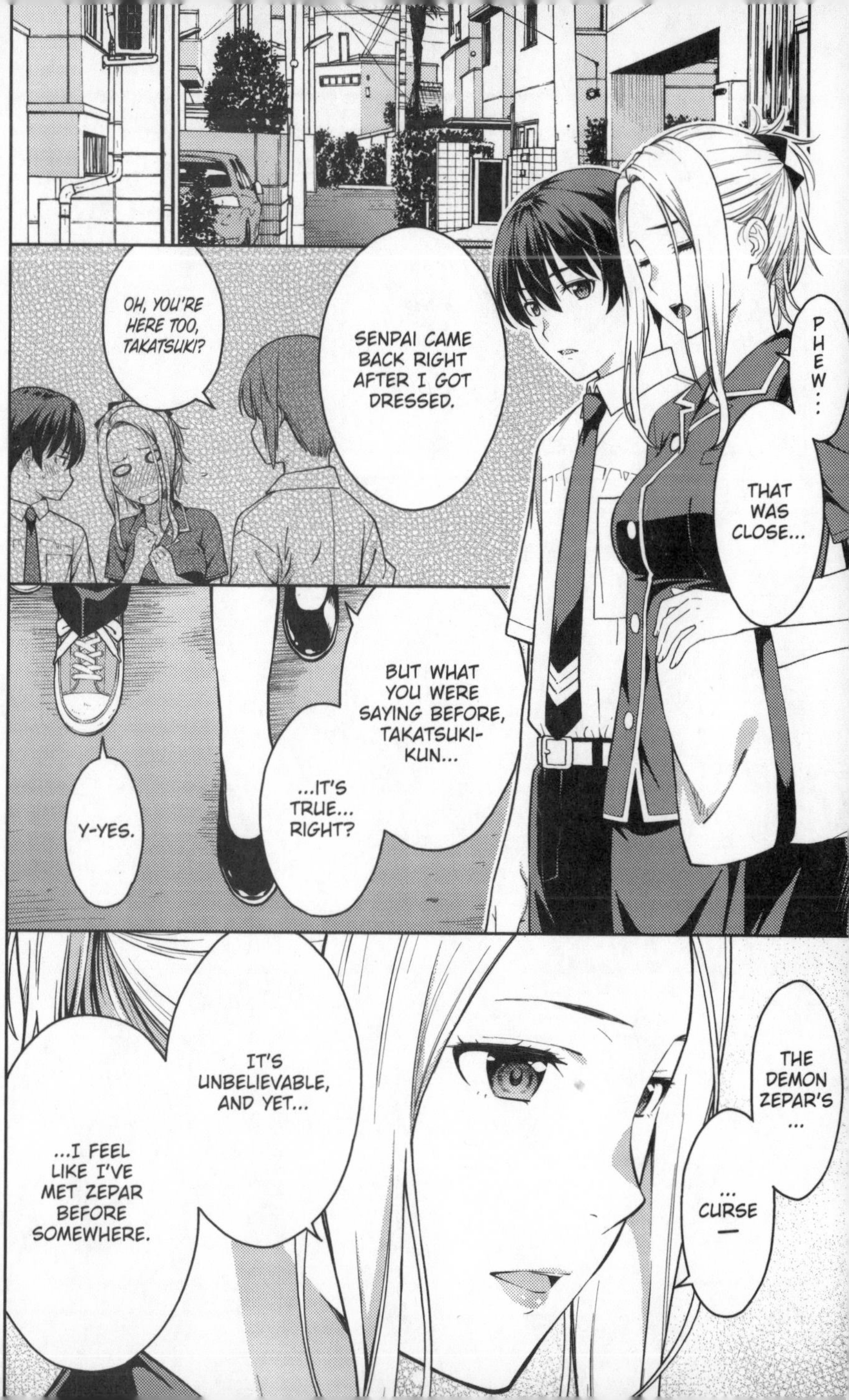
PHEW...
THAT WAS CLOSE...
SENPAI CAME BACK RIGHT AFTER I GOT DRESSED.
OH, YOU'RE HERE TOO, TAKATSUKI?
BUT WHAT YOU WERE SAYING BEFORE, TAKATSUKI-KUN...
...IT'S TRUE... RIGHT?
Y-YES.
THE DEMON ZEPAR'S...
...CURSE—
IT'S UNBELIEVABLE, AND YET...
...I FEEL LIKE I'VE MET ZEPAR BEFORE SOMEWHERE.

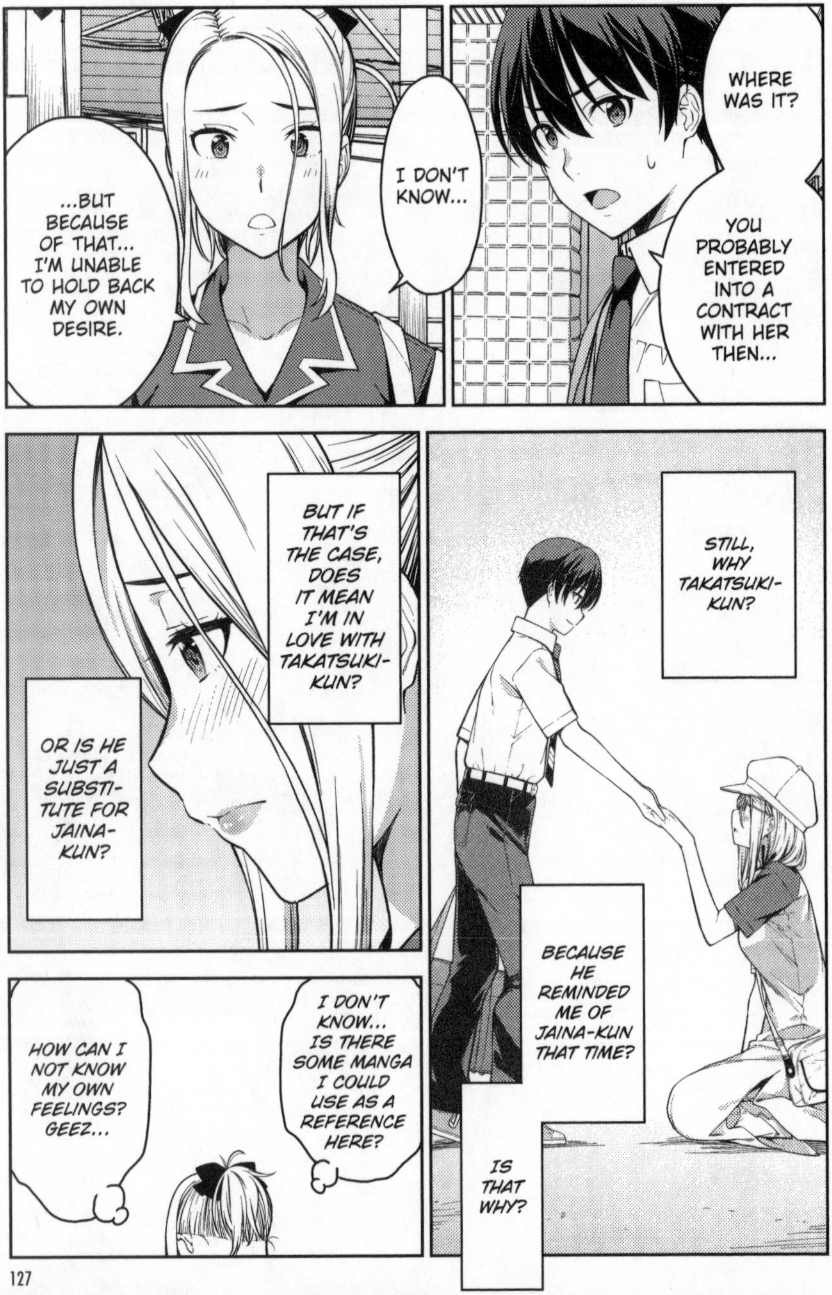
WHERE WAS IT?
YOU PROBABLY ENTERED INTO A CONTRACT WITH HER THEN...
I DON'T KNOW...
...BUT BECAUSE OF THAT... I'M UNABLE TO HOLD BACK MY OWN DESIRE.
STILL, WHY TAKATSUKI-KUN?
BECAUSE HE REMINDED ME OF JAINA-KUN THAT TIME?
IS THAT WHY?
BUT IF THAT'S THE CASE, DOES IT MEAN I'M IN LOVE WITH TAKATSUKI-KUN?
OR IS HE JUST A SUBSTITUTE FOR JAINA-KUN?
I DON'T KNOW... IS THERE SOME MANGA I COULD USE AS A REFERENCE HERE?
HOW CAN I NOT KNOW MY OWN FEELINGS? GEEZ...

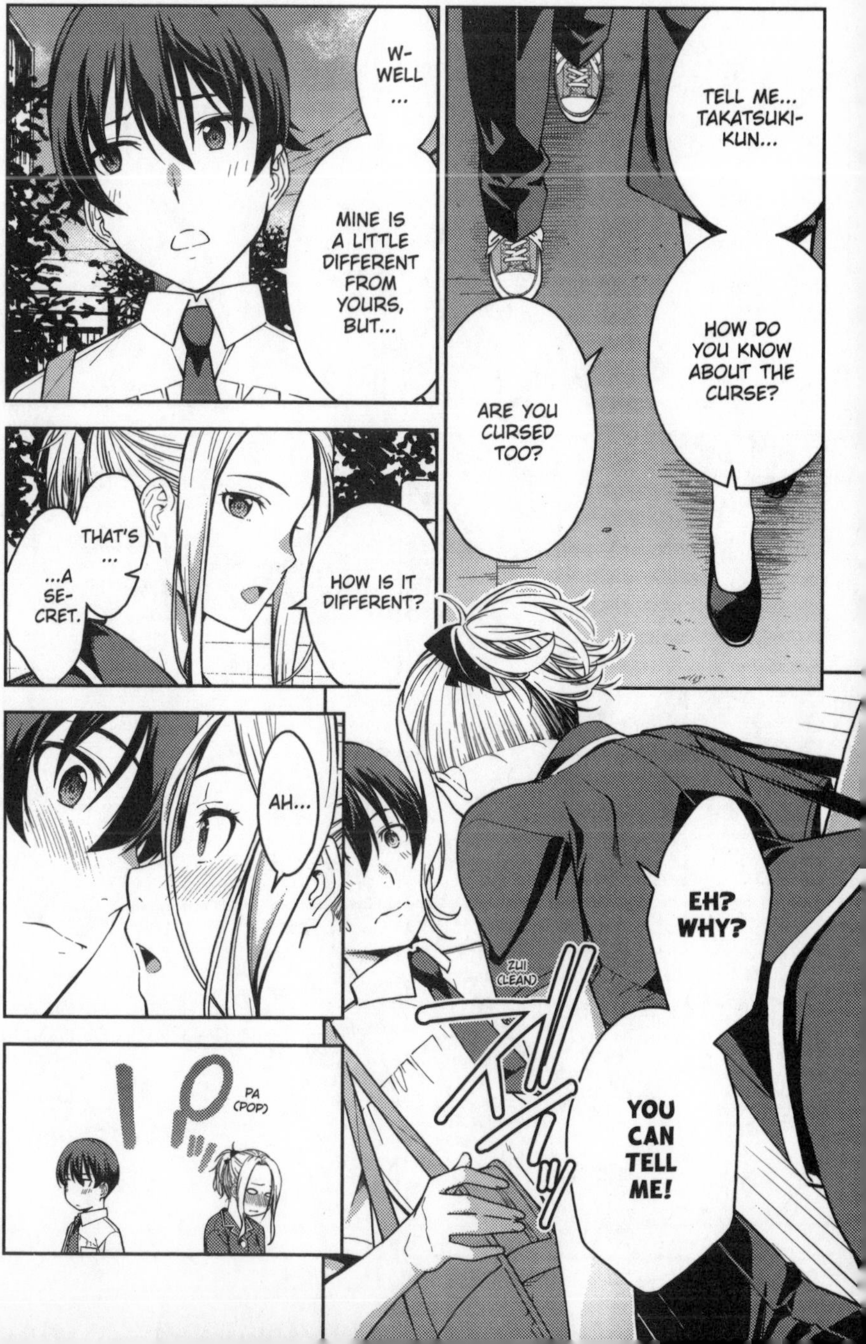
TELL ME... TAKATSUKI-KUN...
HOW DO YOU KNOW ABOUT THE CURSE?
ARE YOU CURSED TOO?
W-WELL...
MINE IS A LITTLE DIFFERENT FROM YOURS, BUT...
HOW IS IT DIFFERENT?
THAT'S...
...A SE-CRET.
EH? WHY?
ZUI (LEAN)
YOU CAN TELL ME!
AH...
PA (POP)

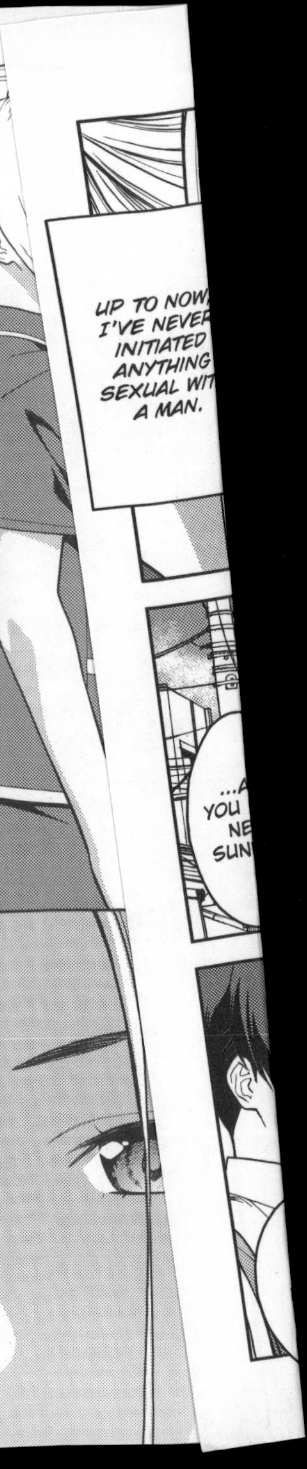
UP TO NOW, I'VE NEVER INITIATED ANYTHING SEXUAL WIT A MAN.
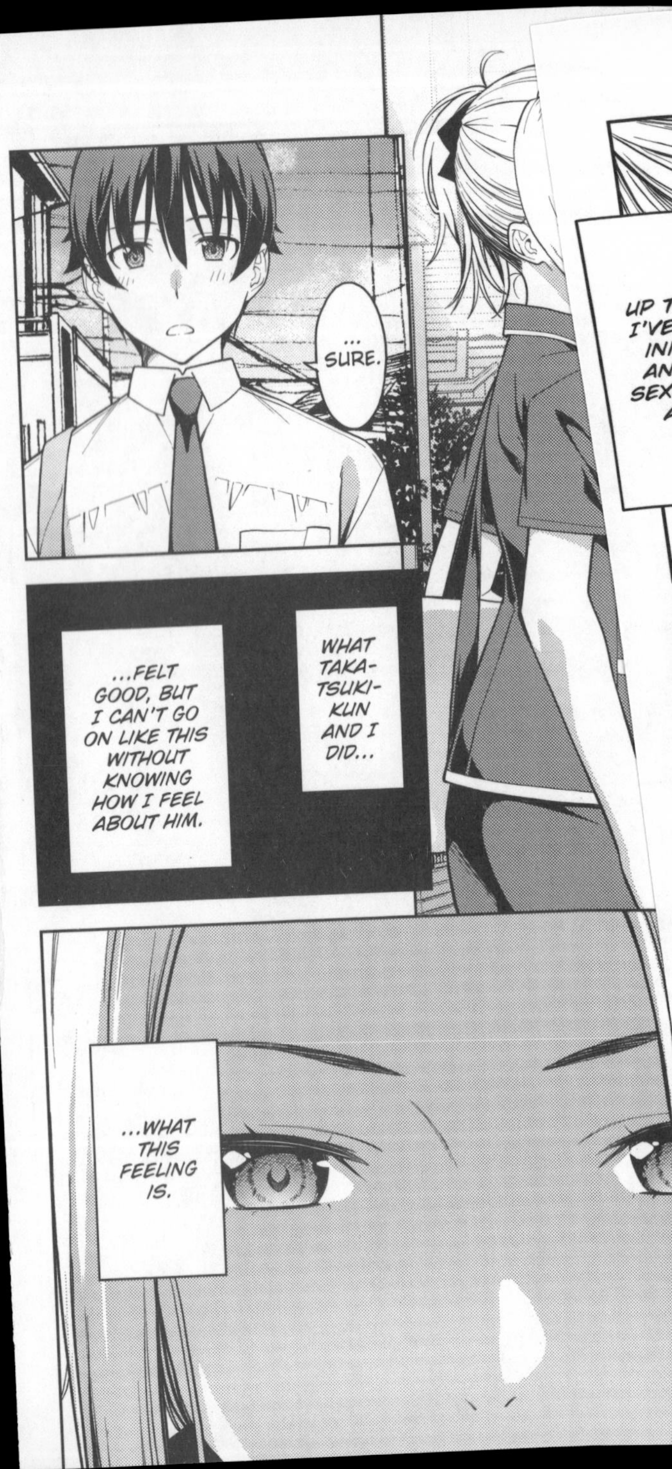
... SURE.
WHAT TAKA-TSUKI-KUN AND I DID...
...FELT GOOD, BUT I CAN'T GO ON LIKE THIS WITHOUT KNOWING HOW I FEEL ABOUT HIM.
...WHAT THIS FEELING IS.
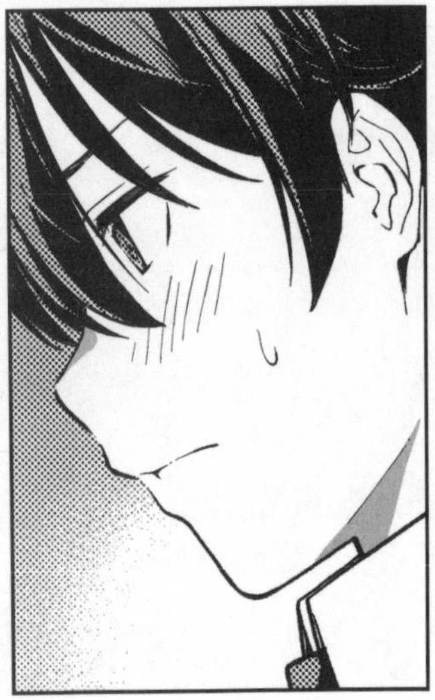

A-ANYWAY—!
THANK YOU FOR TELLING ME ABOUT THE CURSE.
TAKATSUKI-KUN, GOING BY WHAT YOU SAID... IT SEEMS LIKE WE'LL HAVE TO DO THAT AGAIN.
UNTIL THE CURSE IS BROKEN.
DOES THAT MEAN I'M IN LOVE WITH TAKATSUKI-KUN...?
SO...
Y-YES.
EH...?
YES, BUT...

LUST GEASS

Chapter 17

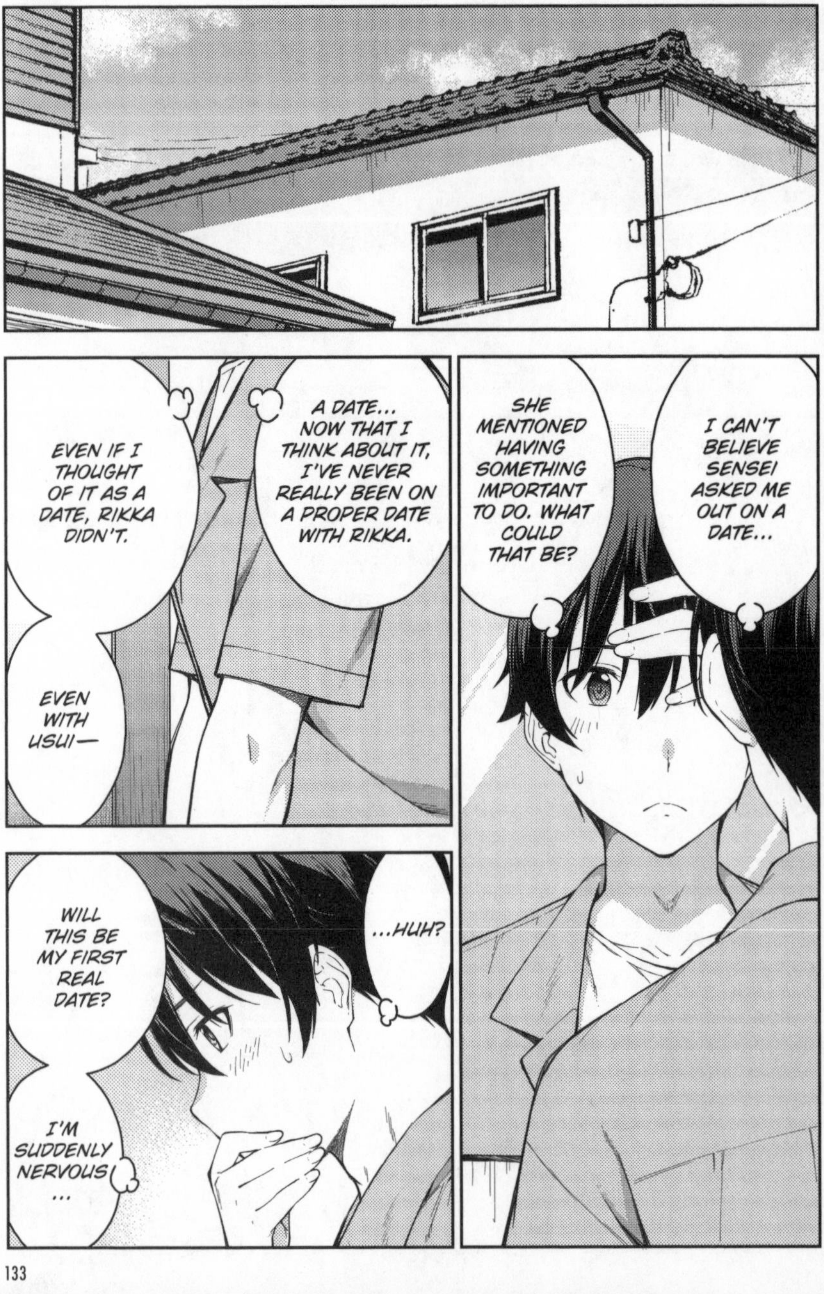

I CAN'T BELIEVE SENSEI ASKED ME OUT ON A DATE...
SHE MENTIONED HAVING SOMETHING IMPORTANT TO DO. WHAT COULD THAT BE?
A DATE... NOW THAT I THINK ABOUT IT, I'VE NEVER REALLY BEEN ON A PROPER DATE WITH RIKKA.
EVEN IF I THOUGHT OF IT AS A DATE, RIKKA DIDN'T.
EVEN WITH USUI—
...HUH?
WILL THIS BE MY FIRST REAL DATE?
I'M SUDDENLY NERVOUS...

SIGNS: SALANPAS / SHIBUYA STATION

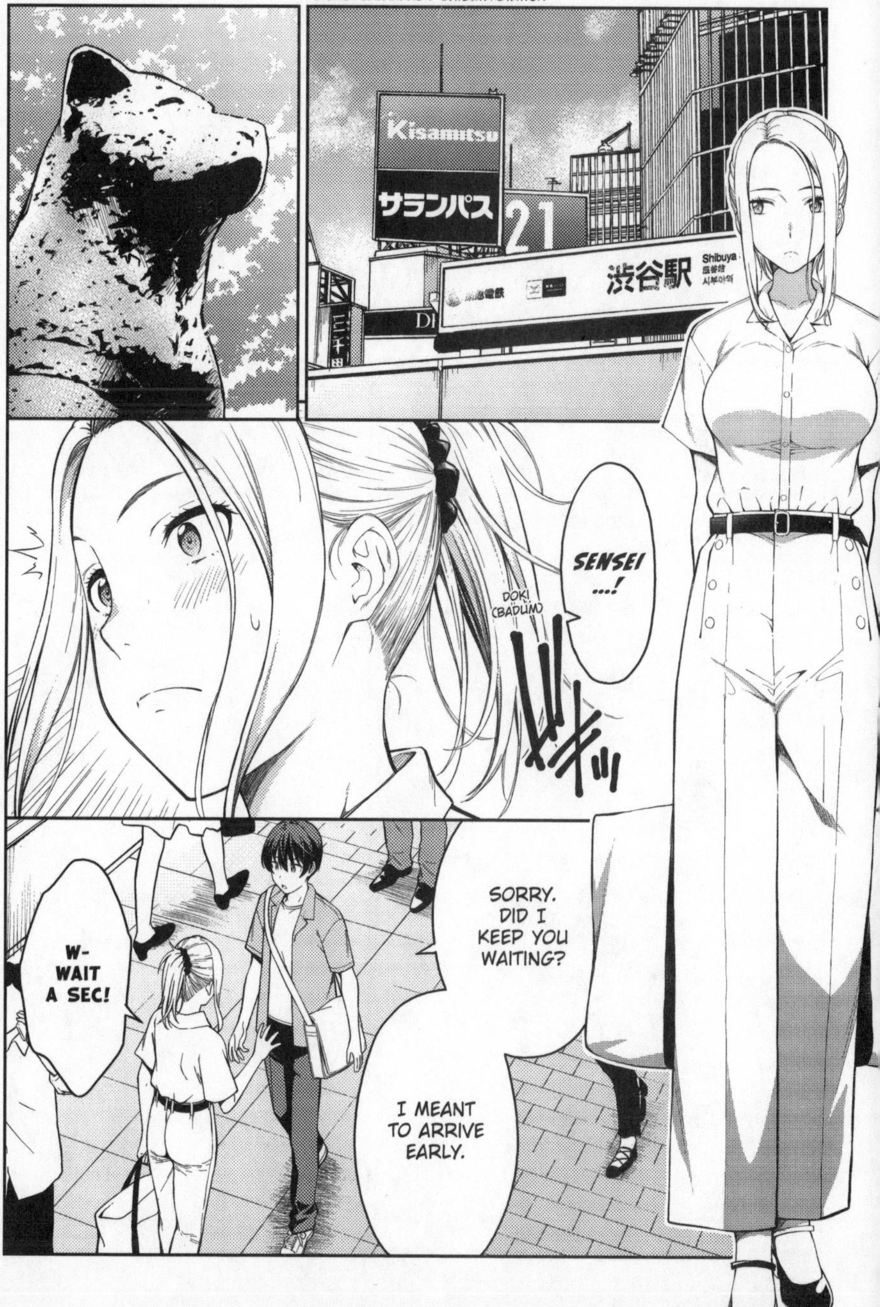
Kisamitsu
サランパス
21
渋谷駅
Shibuya
SENSEI ...!
DOKI (BADUM)
SORRY. DID I KEEP YOU WAITING?
I MEANT TO ARRIVE EARLY.
W-WAIT A SEC!

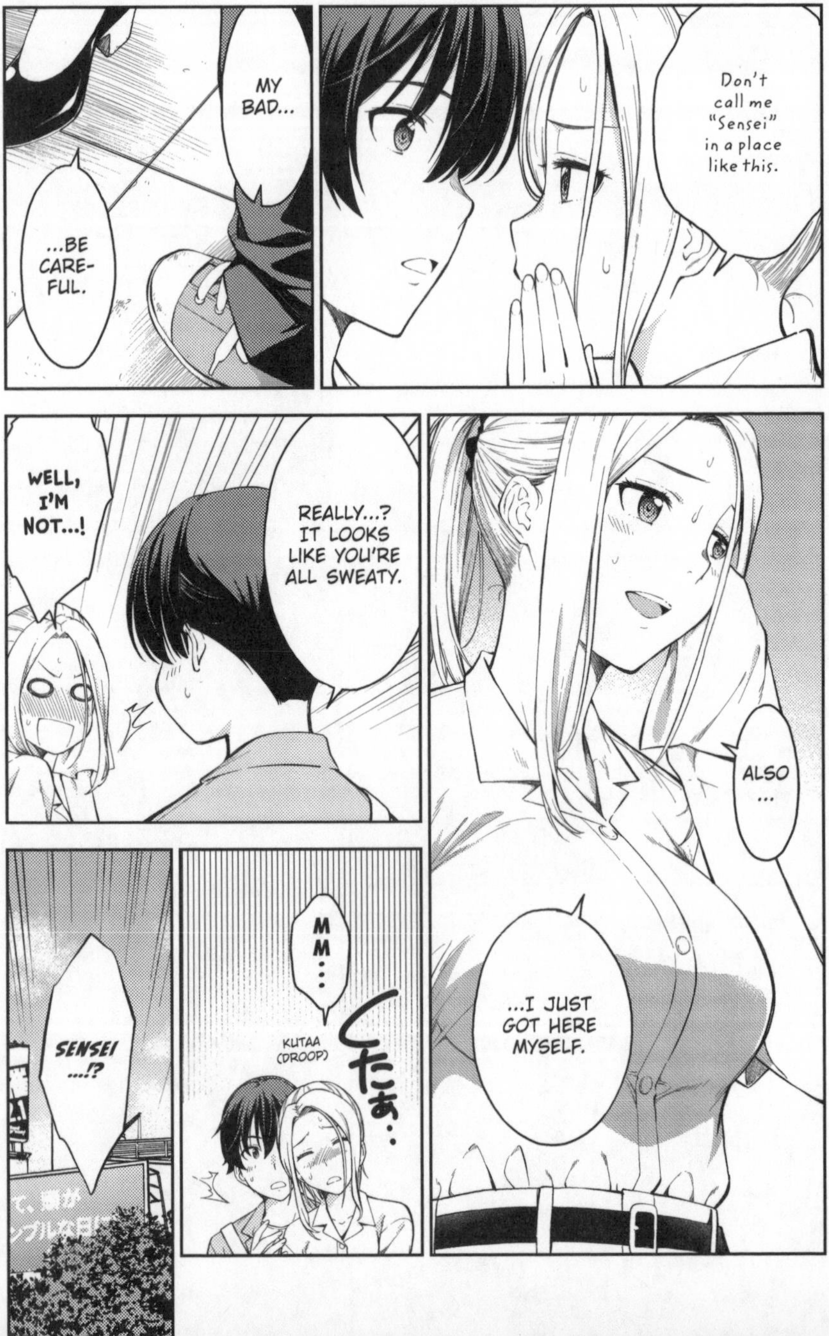
Don't call me "Sensei" in a place like this.
MY BAD...
...BE CARE-FUL.
ALSO...
...I JUST GOT HERE MYSELF.
REALLY...? IT LOOKS LIKE YOU'RE ALL SWEATY.
WELL, I'M NOT...!
MM...
くたぁ..
KUTAA (DROOP)
SENSEI ...!?

...I'M SORRY.

TO BE HONEST, I WAS WAITING ABOUT AN HOUR...

NO, IT HAD TO BE THERE!

WE SHOULD'VE GONE WITH A DIFFERENT PLACE TO MEET UP.

THAT'S WAY TOO EARLY...

BUT...

...AT LEAST ONCE IN MY LIFE, I WANTED TO HAVE THE KIND OF DATE WHERE YOU MEET IN FRONT OF HACHIKO.

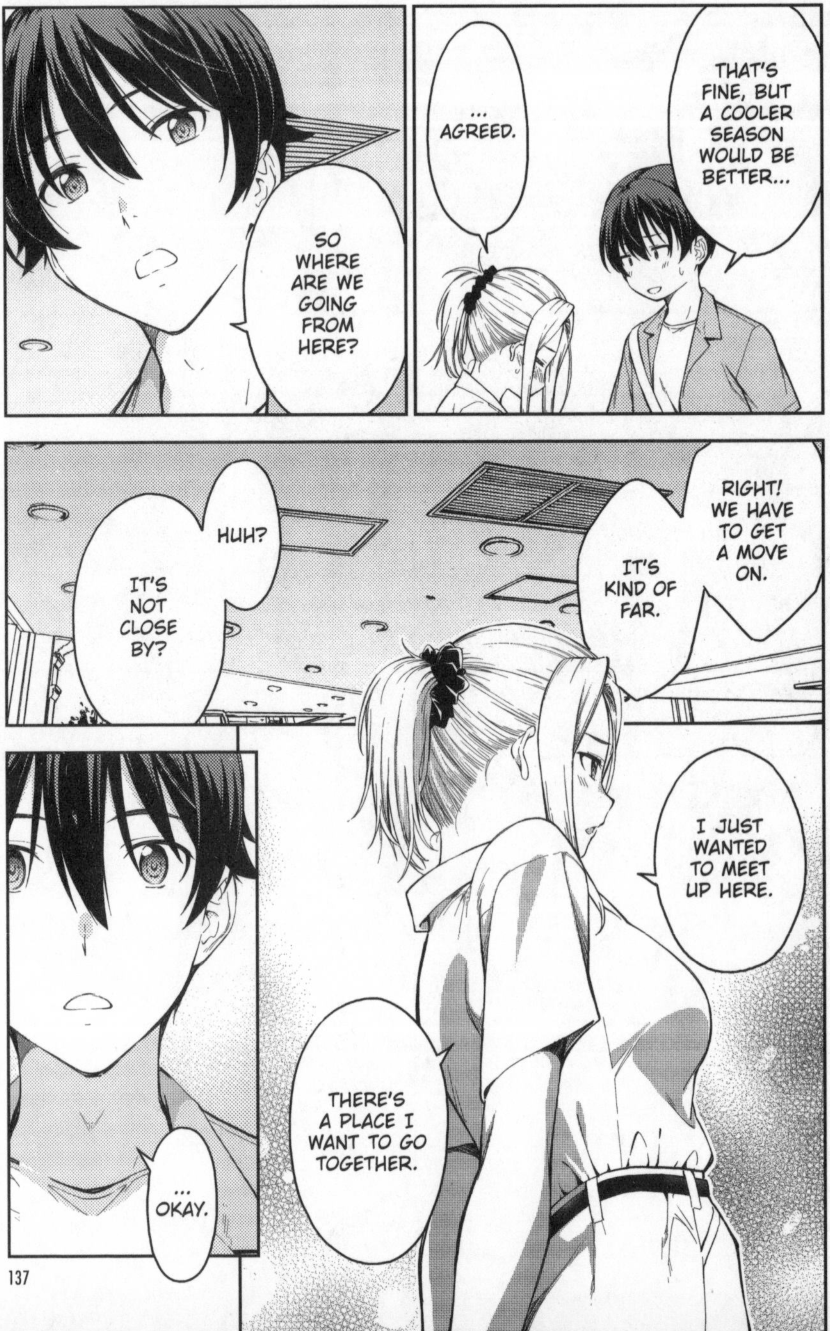
THAT'S FINE, BUT A COOLER SEASON WOULD BE BETTER...
... AGREED.
SO WHERE ARE WE GOING FROM HERE?
RIGHT! WE HAVE TO GET A MOVE ON.
IT'S KIND OF FAR.
HUH?
IT'S NOT CLOSE BY?
I JUST WANTED TO MEET UP HERE.
THERE'S A PLACE I WANT TO GO TOGETHER.
... OKAY.

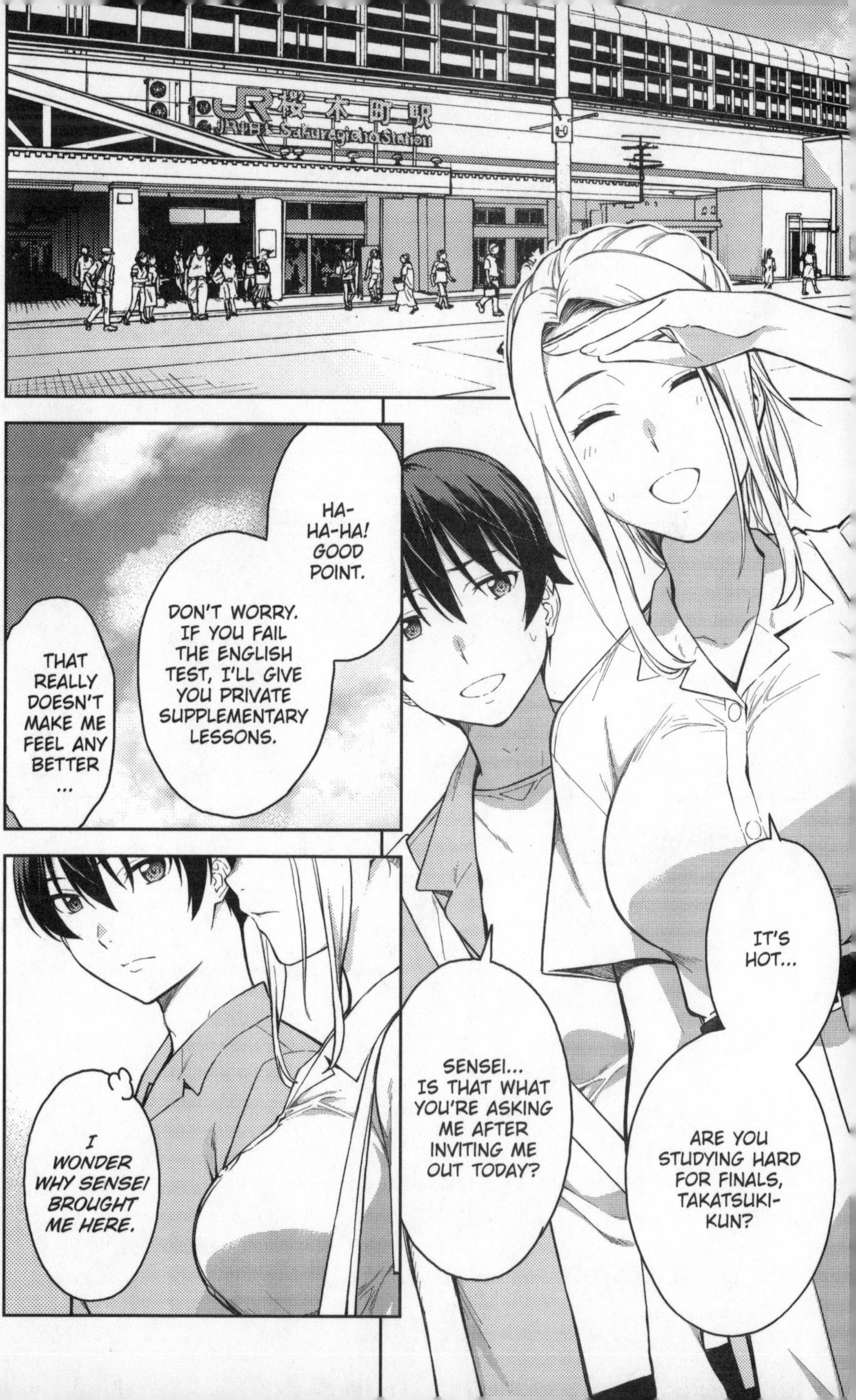
JR 桜木町駅
IT'S HOT...
ARE YOU STUDYING HARD FOR FINALS, TAKATSUKI-KUN?
SENSEI... IS THAT WHAT YOU'RE ASKING ME AFTER INVITING ME OUT TODAY?
HA-HA-HA! GOOD POINT.
DON'T WORRY. IF YOU FAIL THE ENGLISH TEST, I'LL GIVE YOU PRIVATE SUPPLEMENTARY LESSONS.
THAT REALLY DOESN'T MAKE ME FEEL ANY BETTER...
I WONDER WHY SENSEI BROUGHT ME HERE.

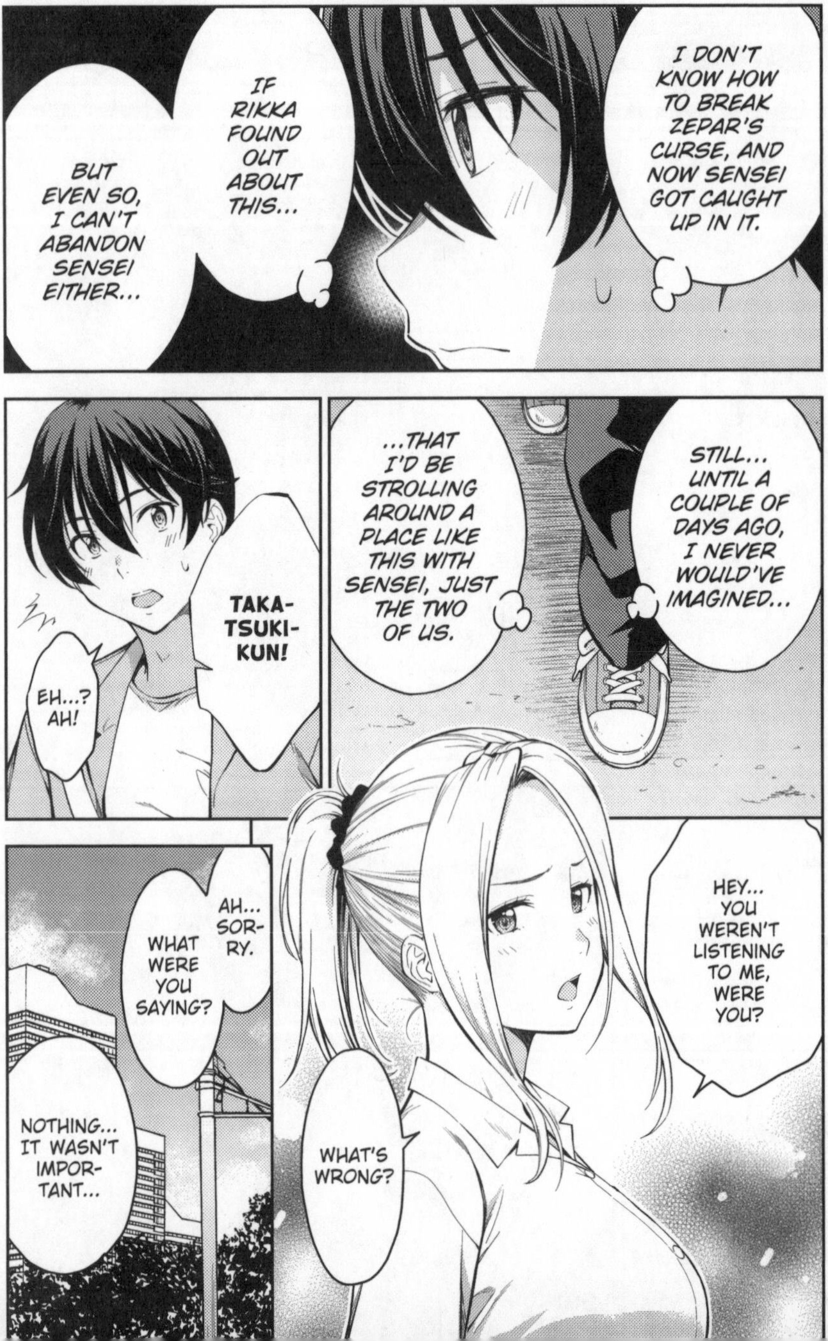
I DON'T KNOW HOW TO BREAK ZEPAR'S CURSE, AND NOW SENSEI GOT CAUGHT UP IN IT.
IF RIKKA FOUND OUT ABOUT THIS...
BUT EVEN SO, I CAN'T ABANDON SENSEI EITHER...
STILL... UNTIL A COUPLE OF DAYS AGO, I NEVER WOULD'VE IMAGINED...
...THAT I'D BE STROLLING AROUND A PLACE LIKE THIS WITH SENSEI, JUST THE TWO OF US.
TAKA-TSUKI-KUN!
EH...? AH!
HEY... YOU WEREN'T LISTENING TO ME, WERE YOU?
WHAT'S WRONG?
AH... SOR-RY.
WHAT WERE YOU SAYING?
NOTHING... IT WASN'T IMPOR-TANT...

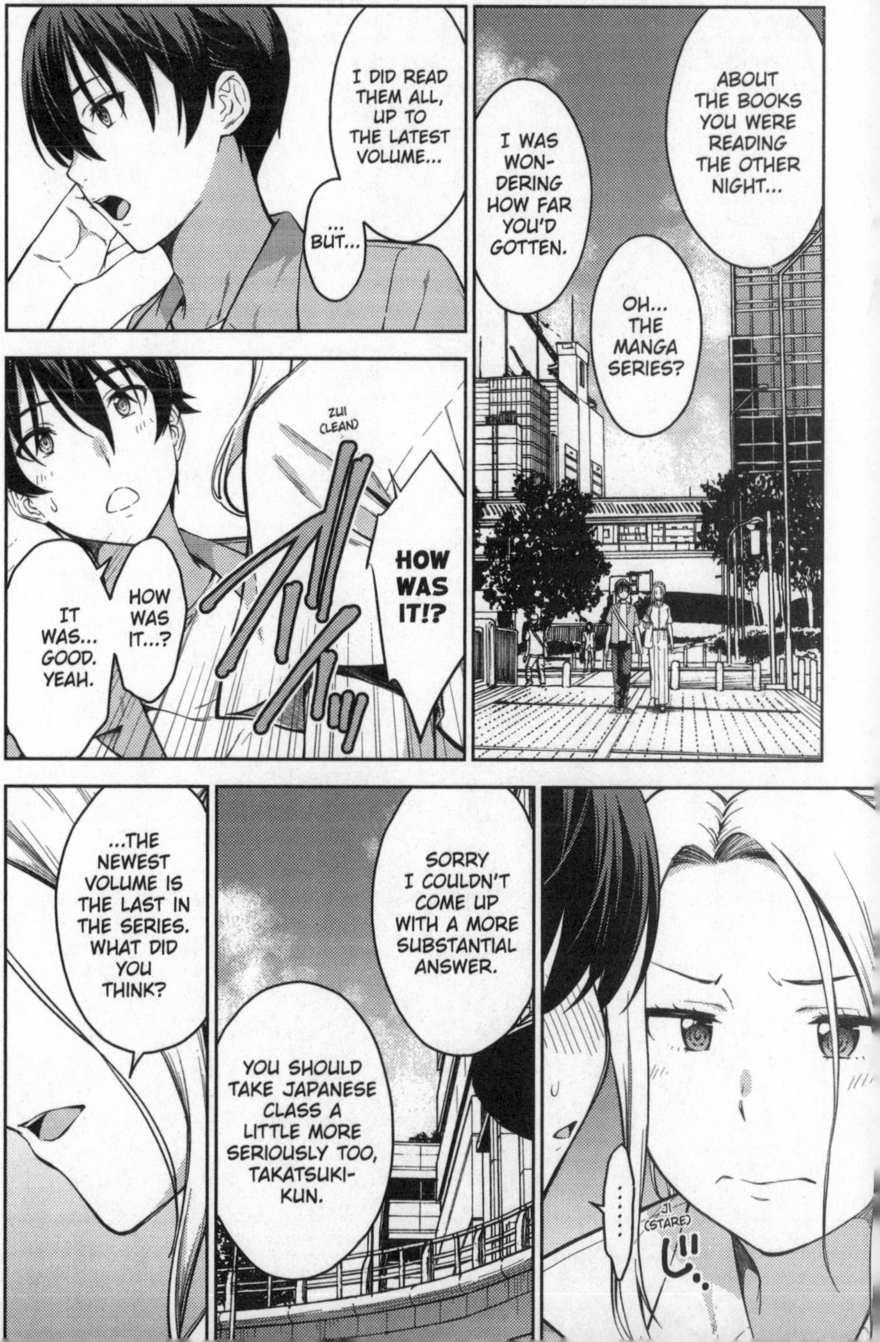
ABOUT THE BOOKS YOU WERE READING THE OTHER NIGHT...
I WAS WONDERING HOW FAR YOU'D GOTTEN.
OH... THE MANGA SERIES?
I DID READ THEM ALL, UP TO THE LATEST VOLUME...
...BUT...
ZUI (LEAN)
HOW WAS IT!?
HOW WAS IT...?
IT WAS... GOOD. YEAH.
......
JI (STARE)
じ...
SORRY I COULDN'T COME UP WITH A MORE SUBSTANTIAL ANSWER.
YOU SHOULD TAKE JAPANESE CLASS A LITTLE MORE SERIOUSLY TOO, TAKATSUKI-KUN.
...THE NEWEST VOLUME IS THE LAST IN THE SERIES. WHAT DID YOU THINK?

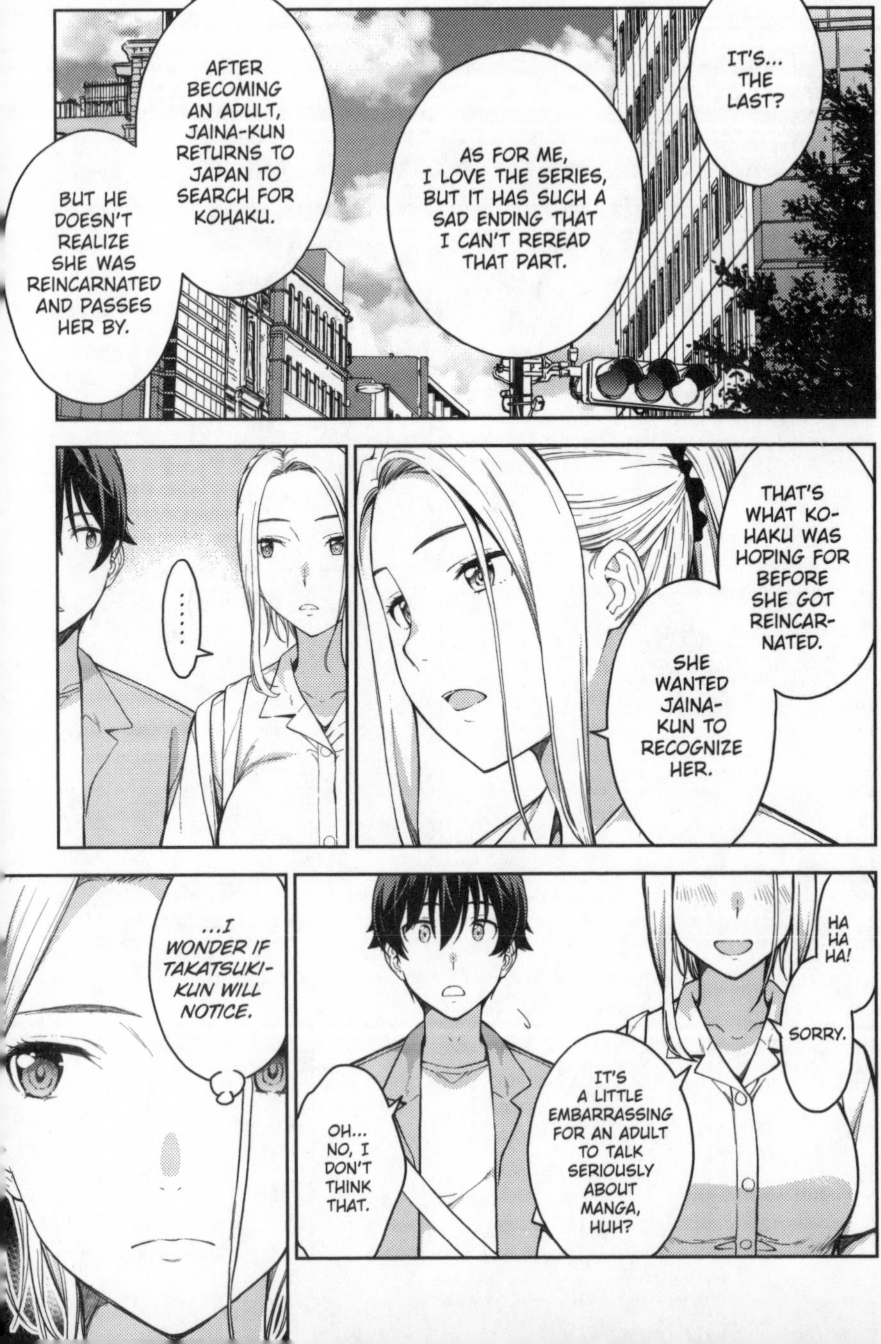
IT'S... THE LAST?
AS FOR ME, I LOVE THE SERIES, BUT IT HAS SUCH A SAD ENDING THAT I CAN'T REREAD THAT PART.
AFTER BECOMING AN ADULT, JAINA-KUN RETURNS TO JAPAN TO SEARCH FOR KOHAKU.
BUT HE DOESN'T REALIZE SHE WAS REINCARNATED AND PASSES HER BY.
THAT'S WHAT KOHAKU WAS HOPING FOR BEFORE SHE GOT REINCARNATED.
SHE WANTED JAINA-KUN TO RECOGNIZE HER.
......
HA HA HA!
SORRY.
IT'S A LITTLE EMBARRASSING FOR AN ADULT TO TALK SERIOUSLY ABOUT MANGA, HUH?
OH... NO, I DON'T THINK THAT.
...I WONDER IF TAKATSUKI-KUN WILL NOTICE.

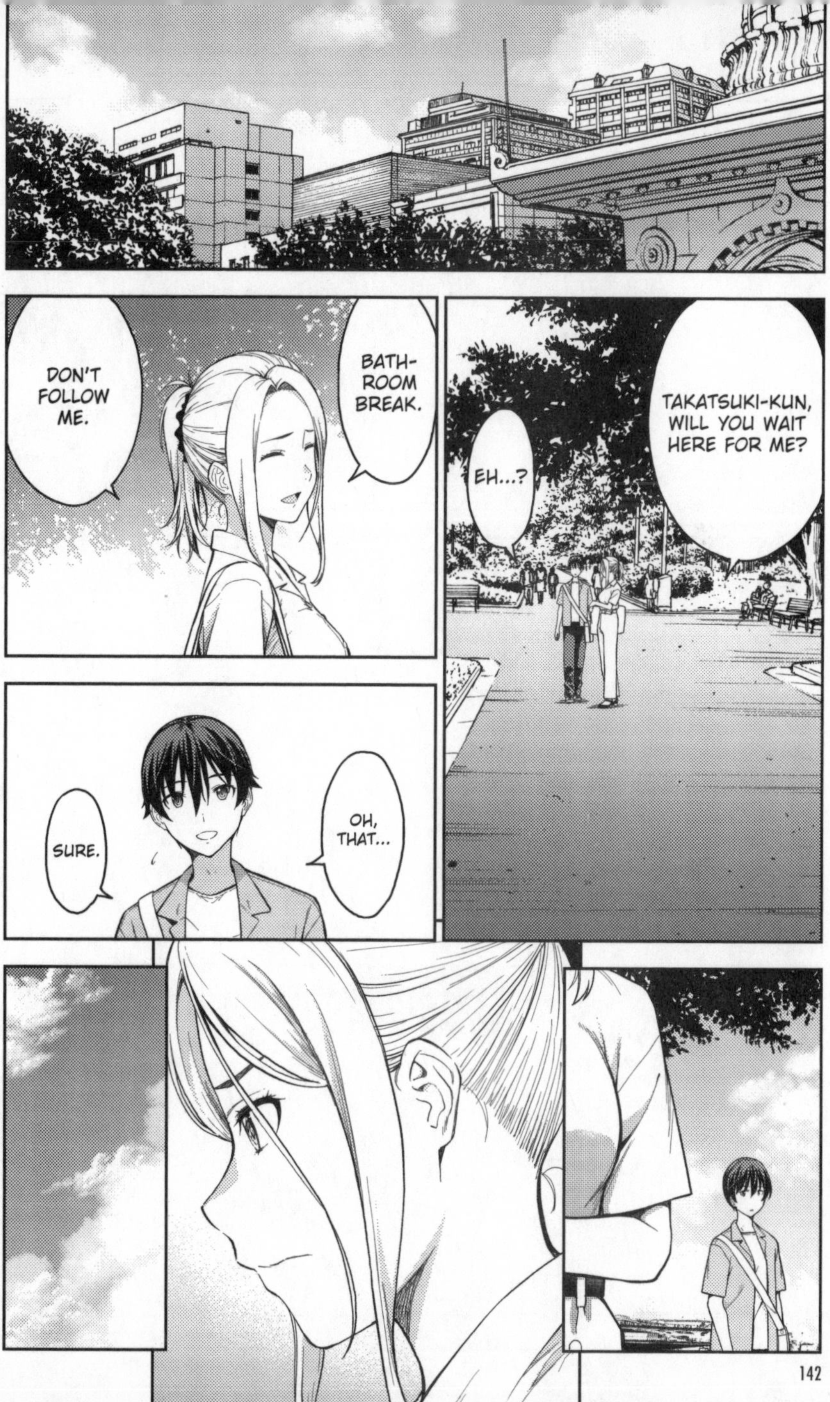
TAKATSUKI-KUN, WILL YOU WAIT HERE FOR ME?
EH...?
BATH-ROOM BREAK.
DON'T FOLLOW ME.
OH, THAT...
SURE.

Sorry, I got lost on the way.

SENSEI?

PURURURU (Bzzzz)

プルルルル

SHE'S BEEN GONE AWHILE NOW...

UM... I'M NOT SURE.

Huh...? Where are you now?

I GUESS SENSEI IS BAD WITH DIRECTIONS ...

STAY WHERE YOU ARE, THEN. I'LL GO LOOK FOR YOU.

Okay. Sorry about this.

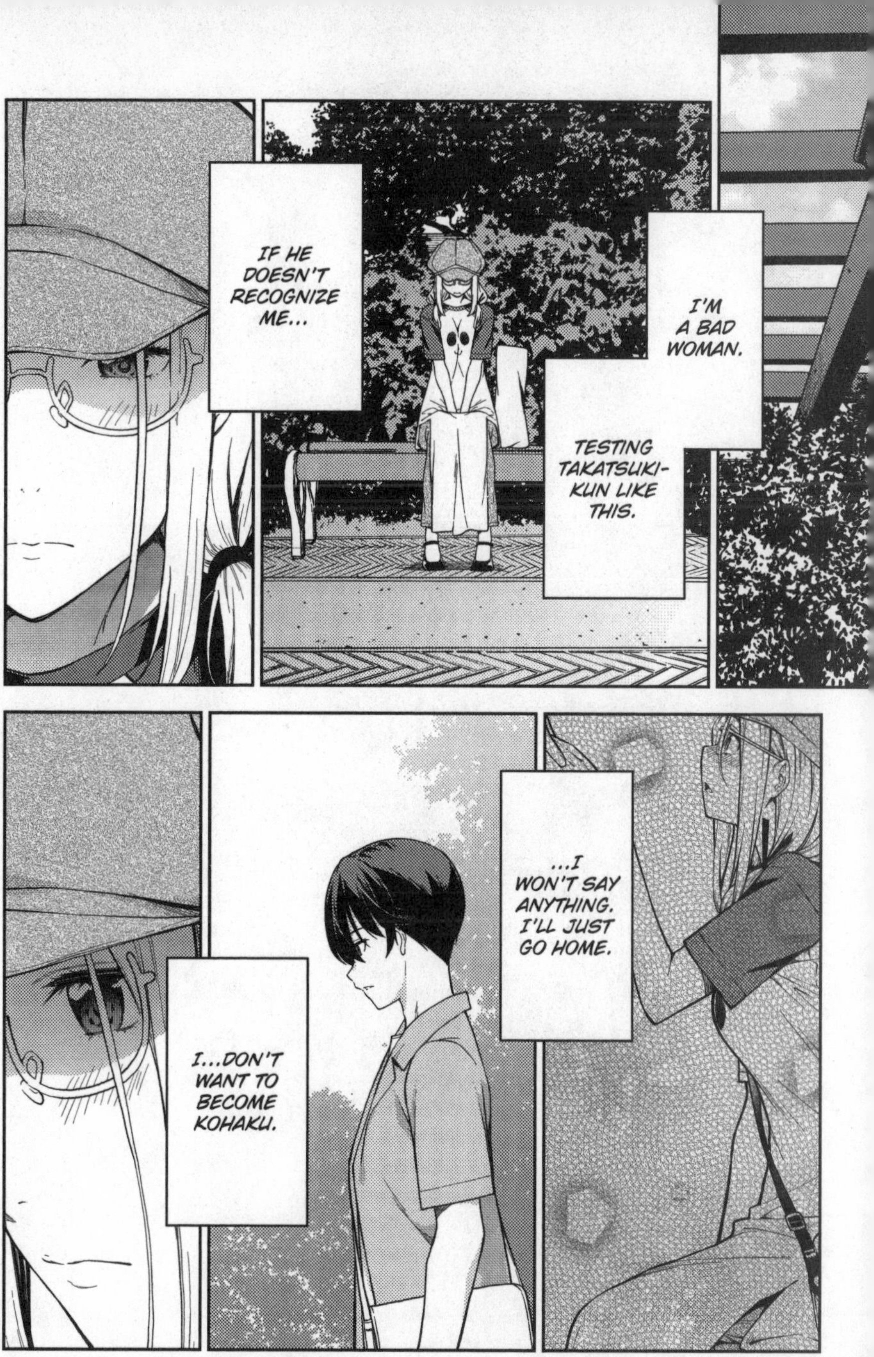
I'M A BAD WOMAN.
TESTING TAKATSUKI-KUN LIKE THIS.
IF HE DOESN'T RECOGNIZE ME...
...I WON'T SAY ANYTHING. I'LL JUST GO HOME.
I...DON'T WANT TO BECOME KOHAKU.

I WANT
HIM TO
REALIZE
IT'S ME.

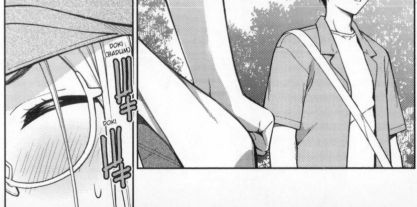

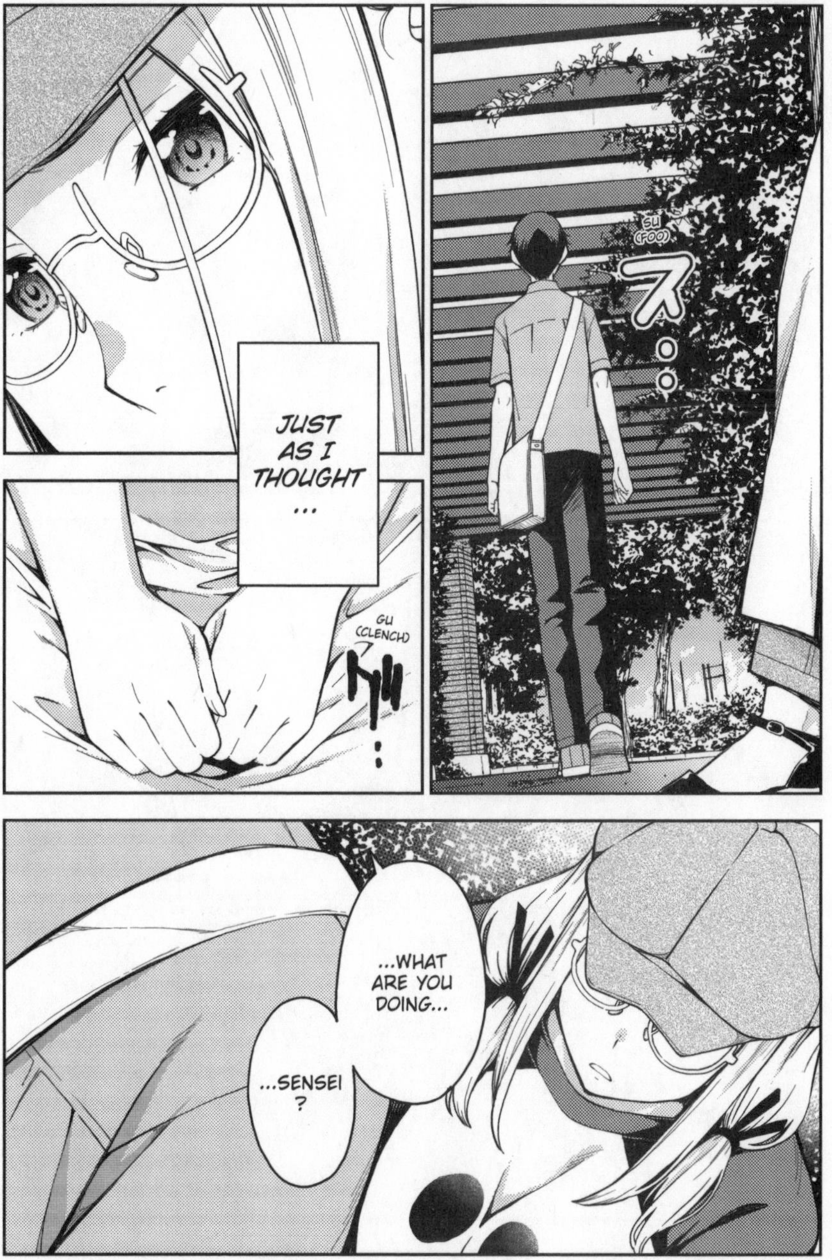
SU (FOO)
JUST AS I THOUGHT...
GU (CLENCH)
...WHAT ARE YOU DOING...
...SENSEI?

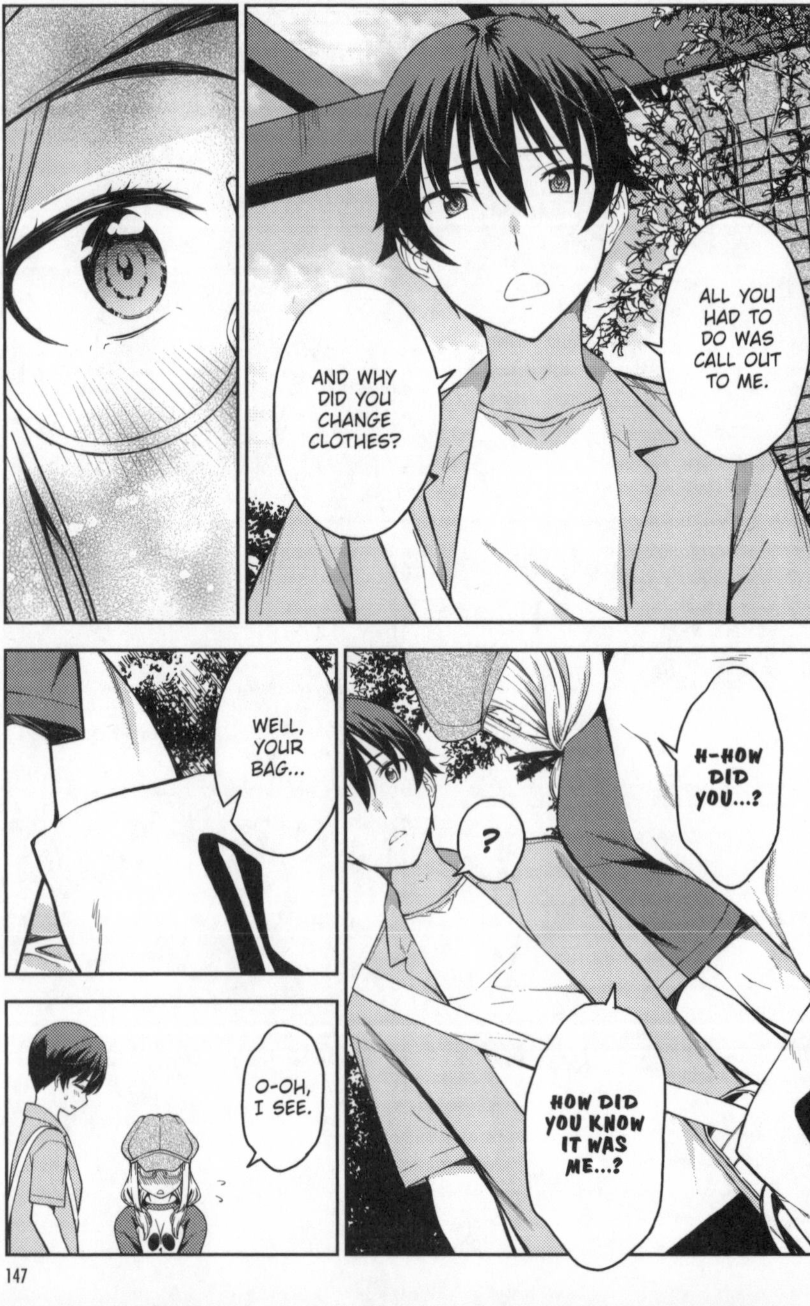
ALL YOU HAD TO DO WAS CALL OUT TO ME.
AND WHY DID YOU CHANGE CLOTHES?
H-HOW DID YOU...?
?
HOW DID YOU KNOW IT WAS ME...?
WELL, YOUR BAG...
O-OH, I SEE.

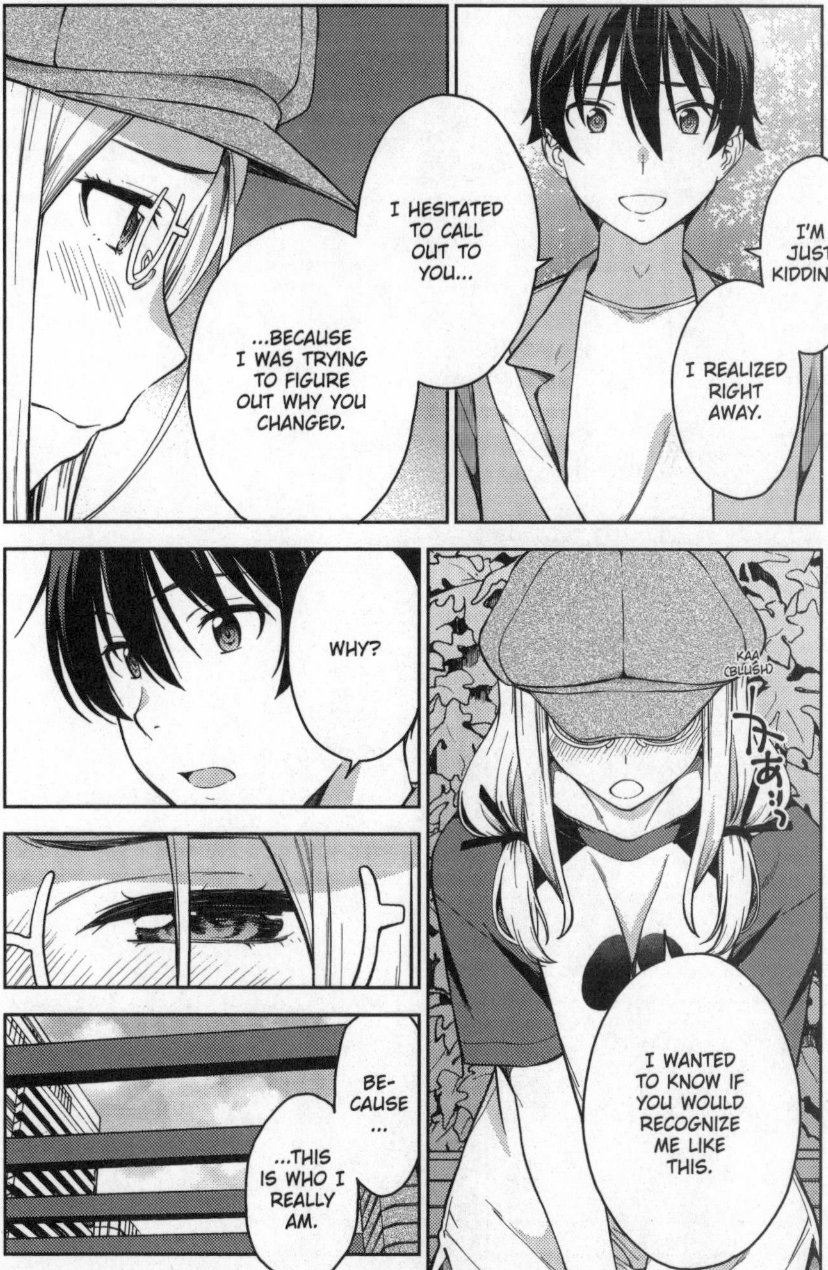
I'M JUST KIDDING.
I REALIZED RIGHT AWAY.
I HESITATED TO CALL OUT TO YOU...
...BECAUSE I WAS TRYING TO FIGURE OUT WHY YOU CHANGED.
KAA (BLUSH)
WHY?
BE-CAUSE ...
...THIS IS WHO I REALLY AM.
I WANTED TO KNOW IF YOU WOULD RECOGNIZE ME LIKE THIS.

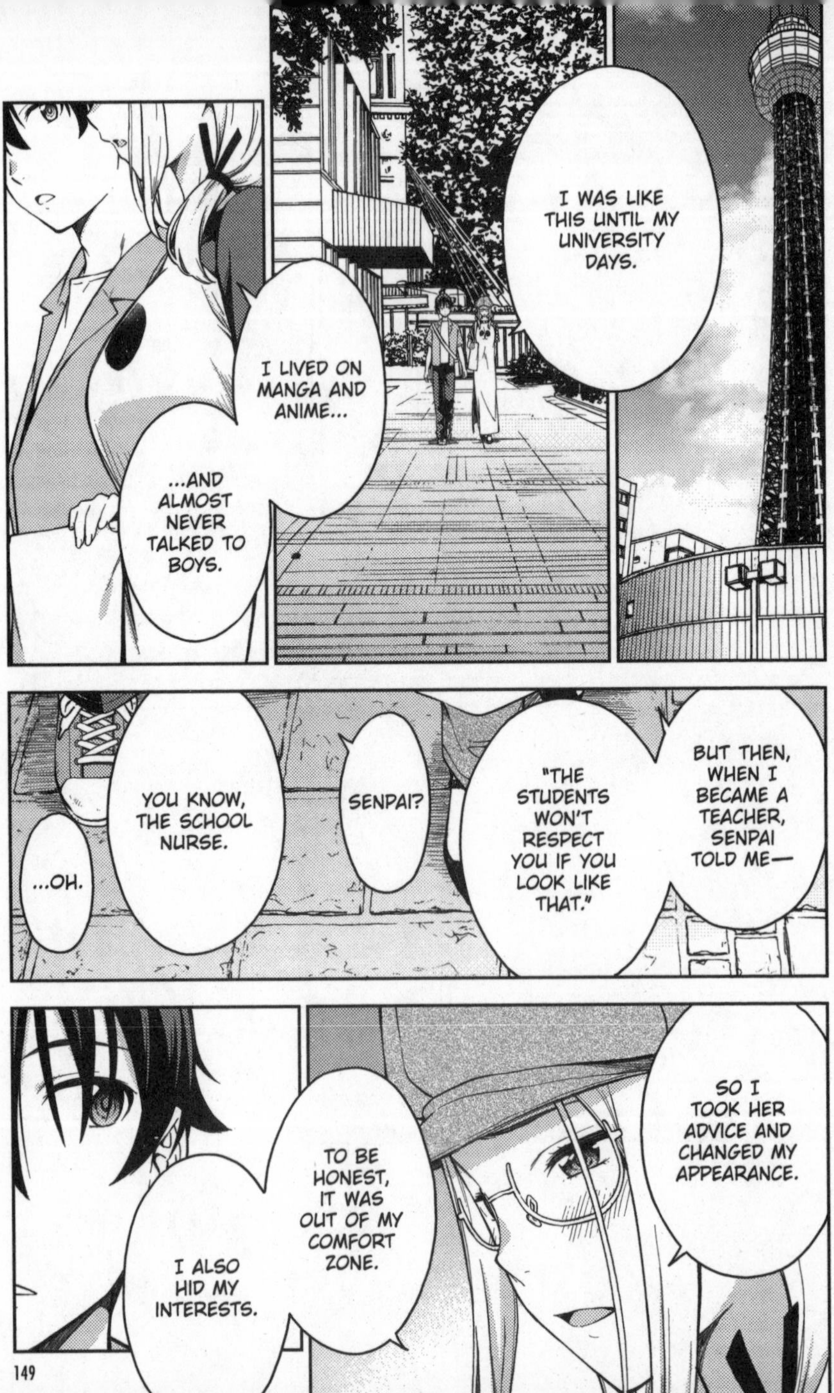
I WAS LIKE THIS UNTIL MY UNIVERSITY DAYS.
I LIVED ON MANGA AND ANIME...
...AND ALMOST NEVER TALKED TO BOYS.
BUT THEN, WHEN I BECAME A TEACHER, SENPAI TOLD ME—
"THE STUDENTS WON'T RESPECT YOU IF YOU LOOK LIKE THAT."
SENPAI?
YOU KNOW, THE SCHOOL NURSE.
...OH.
SO I TOOK HER ADVICE AND CHANGED MY APPEARANCE.
TO BE HONEST, IT WAS OUT OF MY COMFORT ZONE.
I ALSO HID MY INTERESTS.

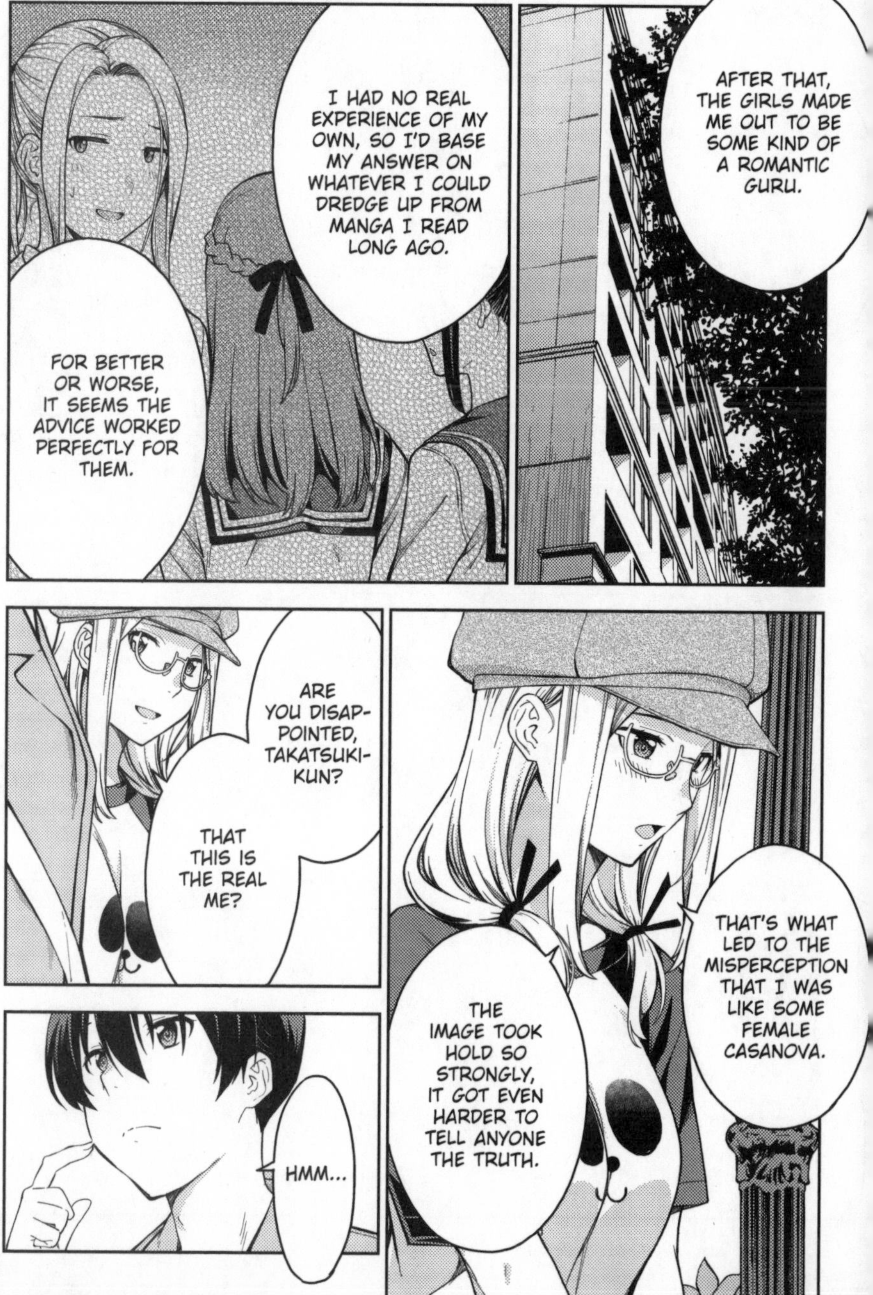
AFTER THAT, THE GIRLS MADE ME OUT TO BE SOME KIND OF A ROMANTIC GURU.
I HAD NO REAL EXPERIENCE OF MY OWN, SO I'D BASE MY ANSWER ON WHATEVER I COULD DREDGE UP FROM MANGA I READ LONG AGO.
FOR BETTER OR WORSE, IT SEEMS THE ADVICE WORKED PERFECTLY FOR THEM.
THAT'S WHAT LED TO THE MISPERCEPTION THAT I WAS LIKE SOME FEMALE CASANOVA.
THE IMAGE TOOK HOLD SO STRONGLY, IT GOT EVEN HARDER TO TELL ANYONE THE TRUTH.
ARE YOU DISAP-POINTED, TAKATSUKI-KUN?
THAT THIS IS THE REAL ME?
HMM...

I LIKE THIS "YOU" TOO, SENSEI.

ISN'T IT FINE IF THEY'RE BOTH REAL?

BESIDES, THE WAY YOU ARE NOW REMINDS ME A LITTLE OF RIKKA, SO IT FEELS FAMILIAR.

NO, I WON'T.

...THAT'S WHAT YOU SAY...

...BUT YOU'LL PROBABLY MAKE FUN OF ME BEHIND MY BACK.

SENSEI, WAIT...!!

AH... SORRY.

IT'S PRETTY INSENSITIVE TO BRING UP ANOTHER GIRL WHEN YOU'RE ON A DATE.

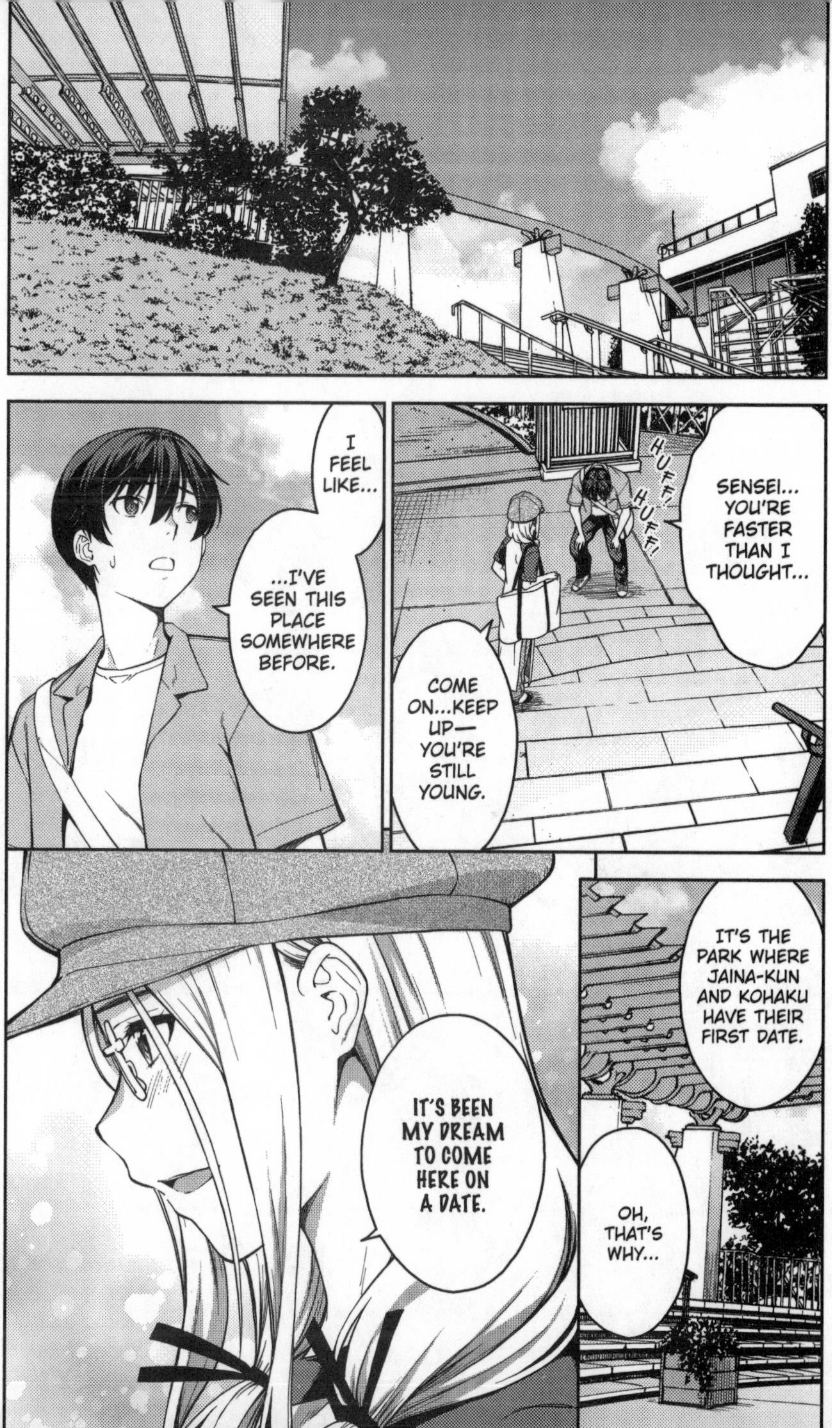
HUFF! HUFF!
SENSEI... YOU'RE FASTER THAN I THOUGHT...
COME ON...KEEP UP—YOU'RE STILL YOUNG.
I FEEL LIKE...
...I'VE SEEN THIS PLACE SOMEWHERE BEFORE.
IT'S THE PARK WHERE JAINA-KUN AND KOHAKU HAVE THEIR FIRST DATE.
OH, THAT'S WHY...
IT'S BEEN MY DREAM TO COME HERE ON A DATE.

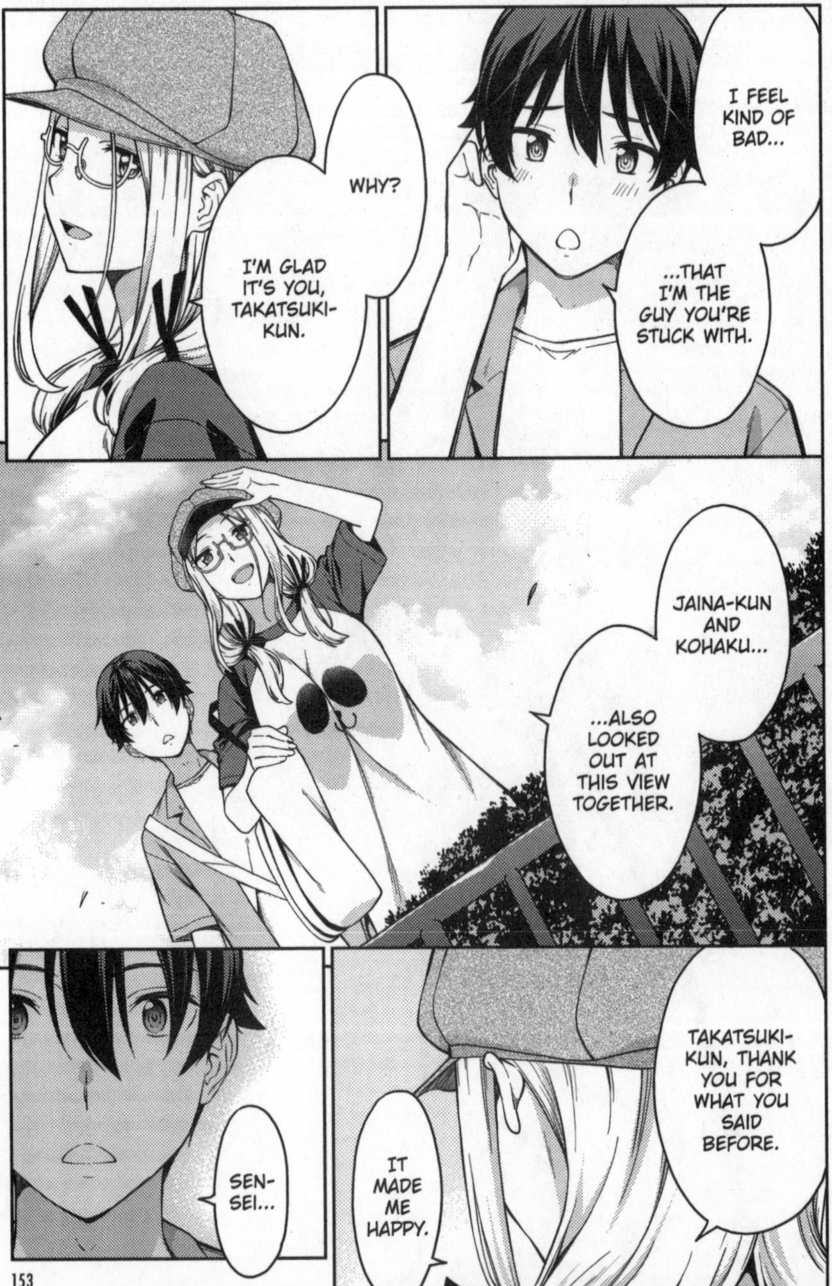
I FEEL KIND OF BAD...
...THAT I'M THE GUY YOU'RE STUCK WITH.
WHY?
I'M GLAD IT'S YOU, TAKATSUKI-KUN.
JAINA-KUN AND KOHAKU...
...ALSO LOOKED OUT AT THIS VIEW TOGETHER.
TAKATSUKI-KUN, THANK YOU FOR WHAT YOU SAID BEFORE.
IT MADE ME HAPPY.
SEN-SEI...

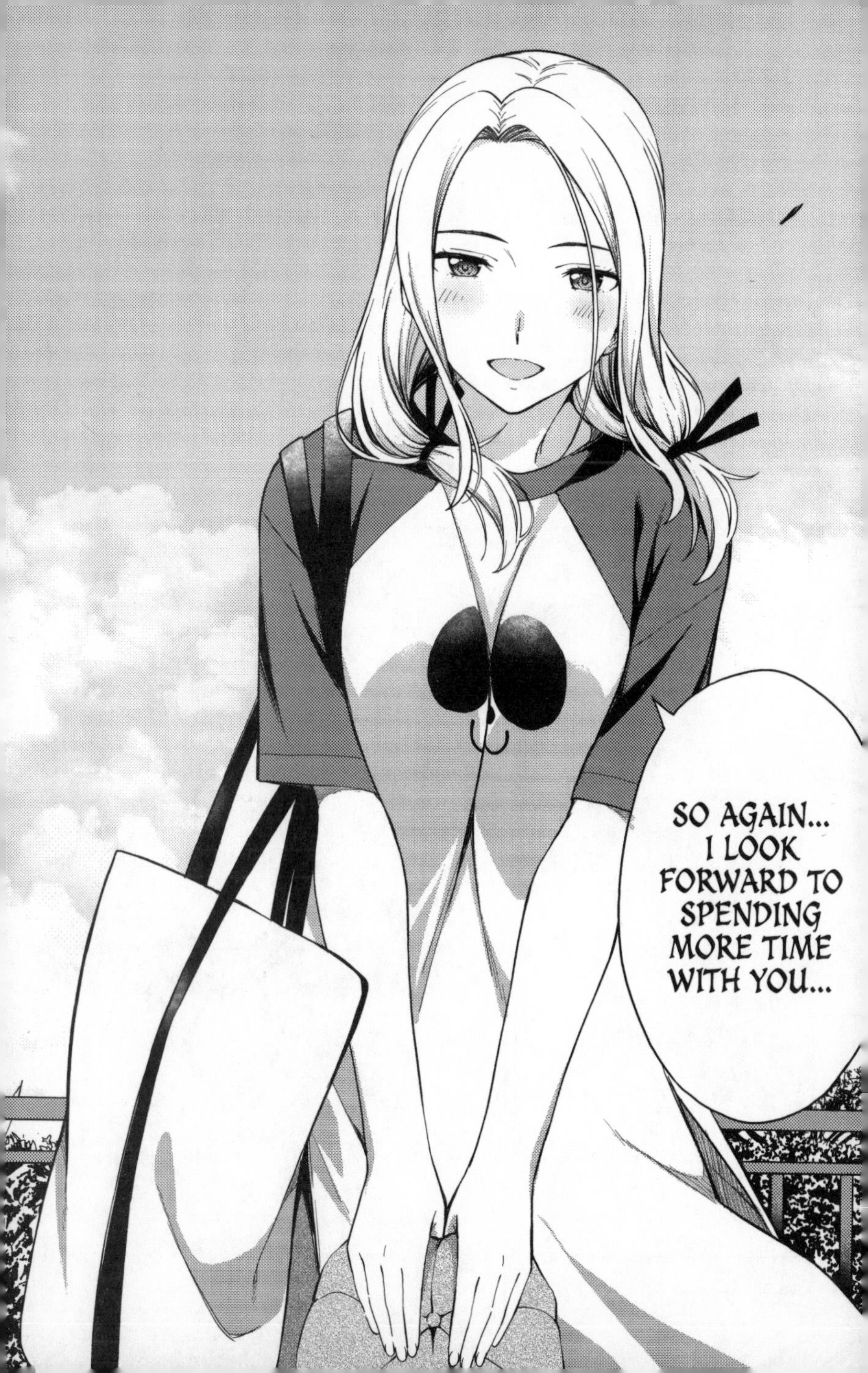
SO AGAIN... I LOOK FORWARD TO SPENDING MORE TIME WITH YOU...

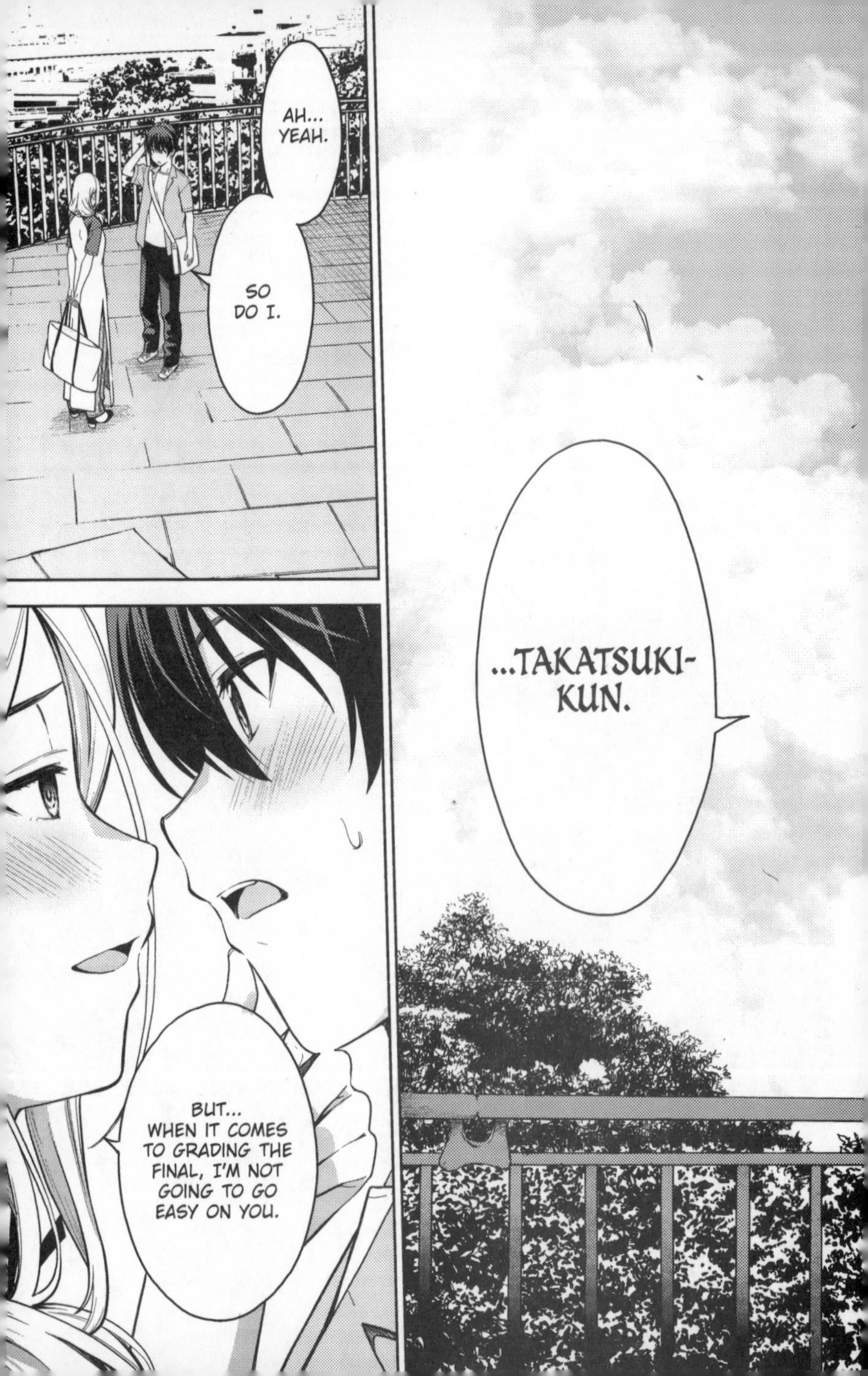
...TAKATSUKI-KUN.
AH... YEAH.
SO DO I.
BUT... WHEN IT COMES TO GRADING THE FINAL, I'M NOT GOING TO GO EASY ON YOU.

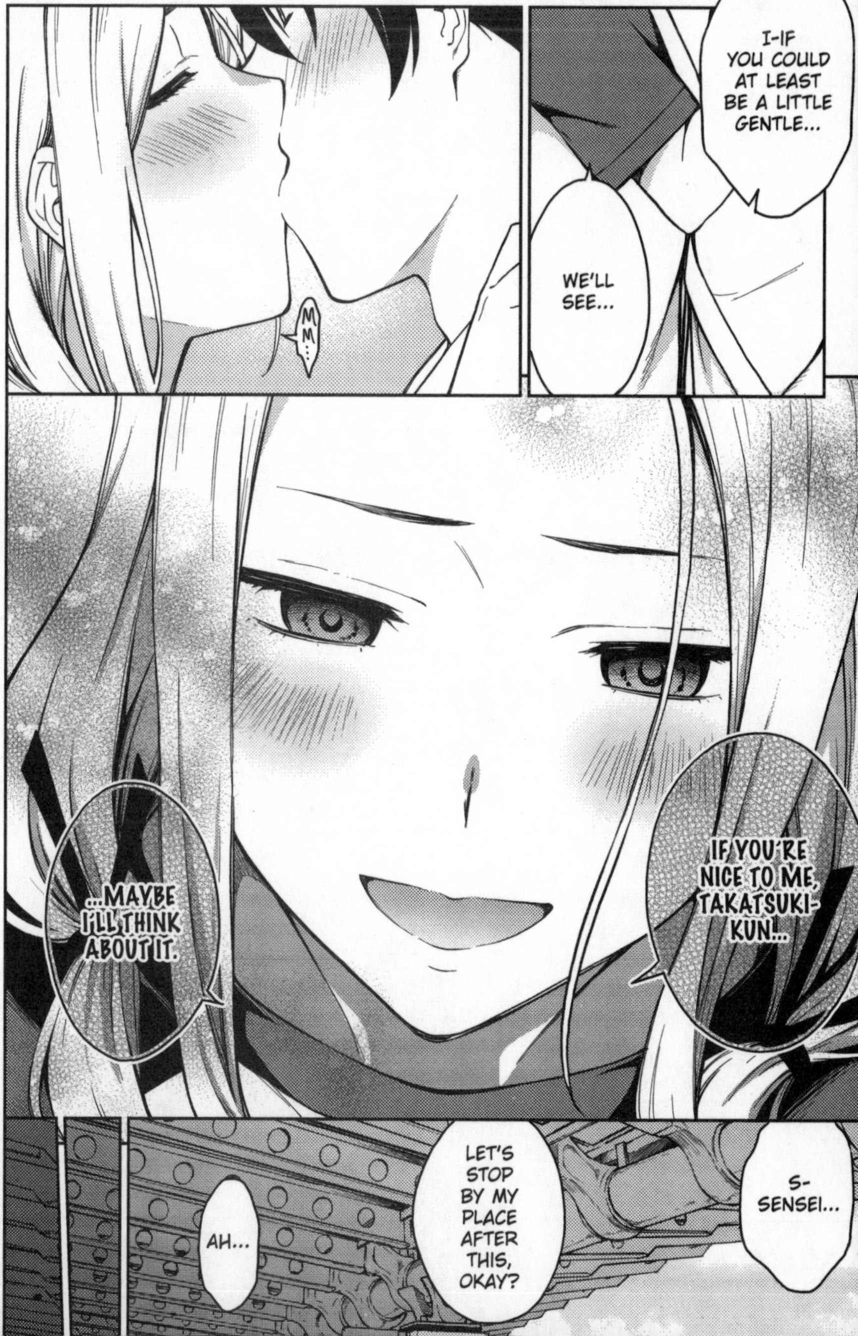
I-IF YOU COULD AT LEAST BE A LITTLE GENTLE...
WE'LL SEE...
MM...
IF YOU'RE NICE TO ME, TAKATSUKI-KUN...
...MAYBE I'LL THINK ABOUT IT.
S-SENSEI...
LET'S STOP BY MY PLACE AFTER THIS, OKAY?
AH...

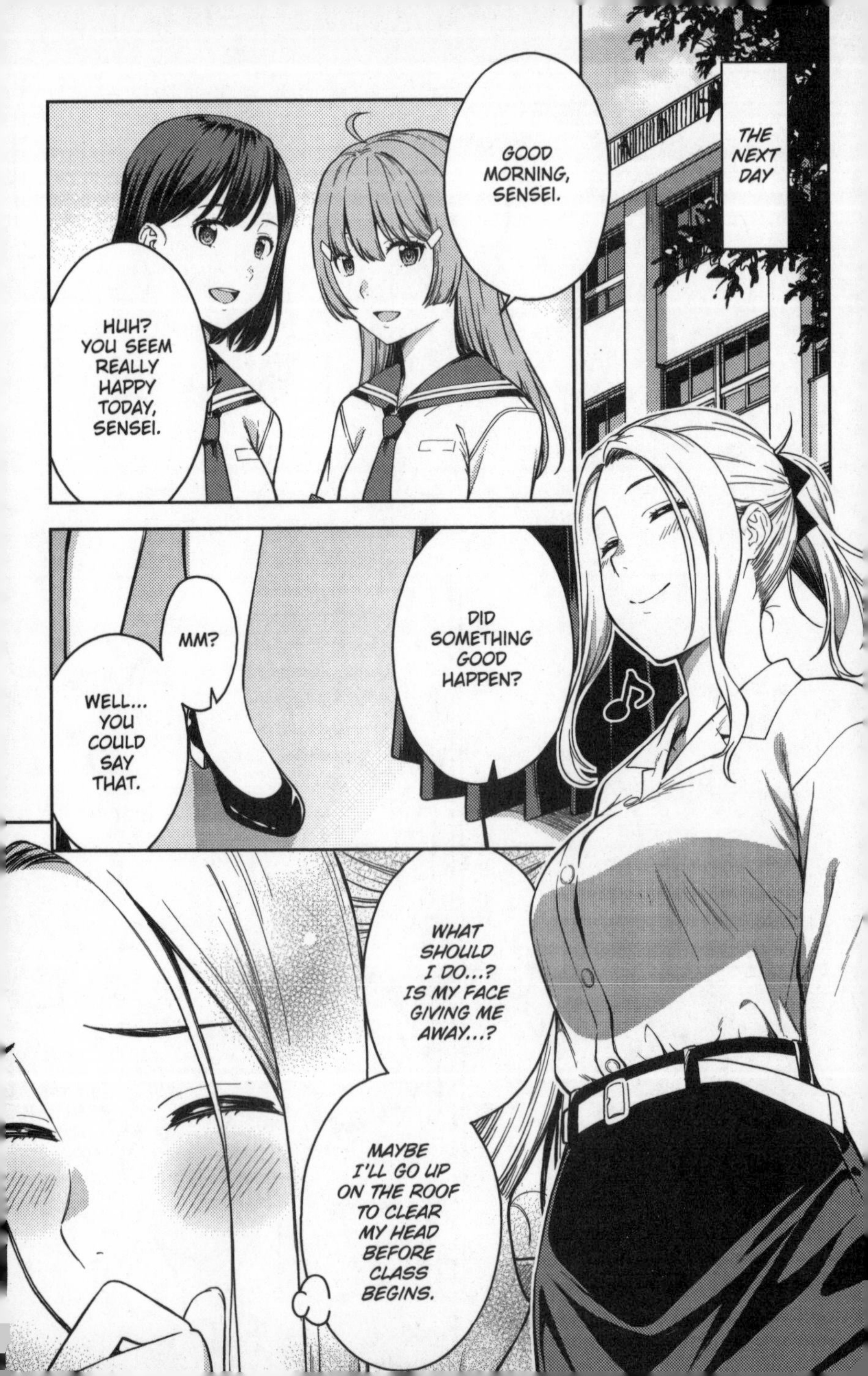
THE NEXT DAY
GOOD MORNING, SENSEI.
HUH? YOU SEEM REALLY HAPPY TODAY, SENSEI.
DID SOMETHING GOOD HAPPEN?
MM?
WELL... YOU COULD SAY THAT.
WHAT SHOULD I DO...? IS MY FACE GIVING ME AWAY...?
MAYBE I'LL GO UP ON THE ROOF TO CLEAR MY HEAD BEFORE CLASS BEGINS.

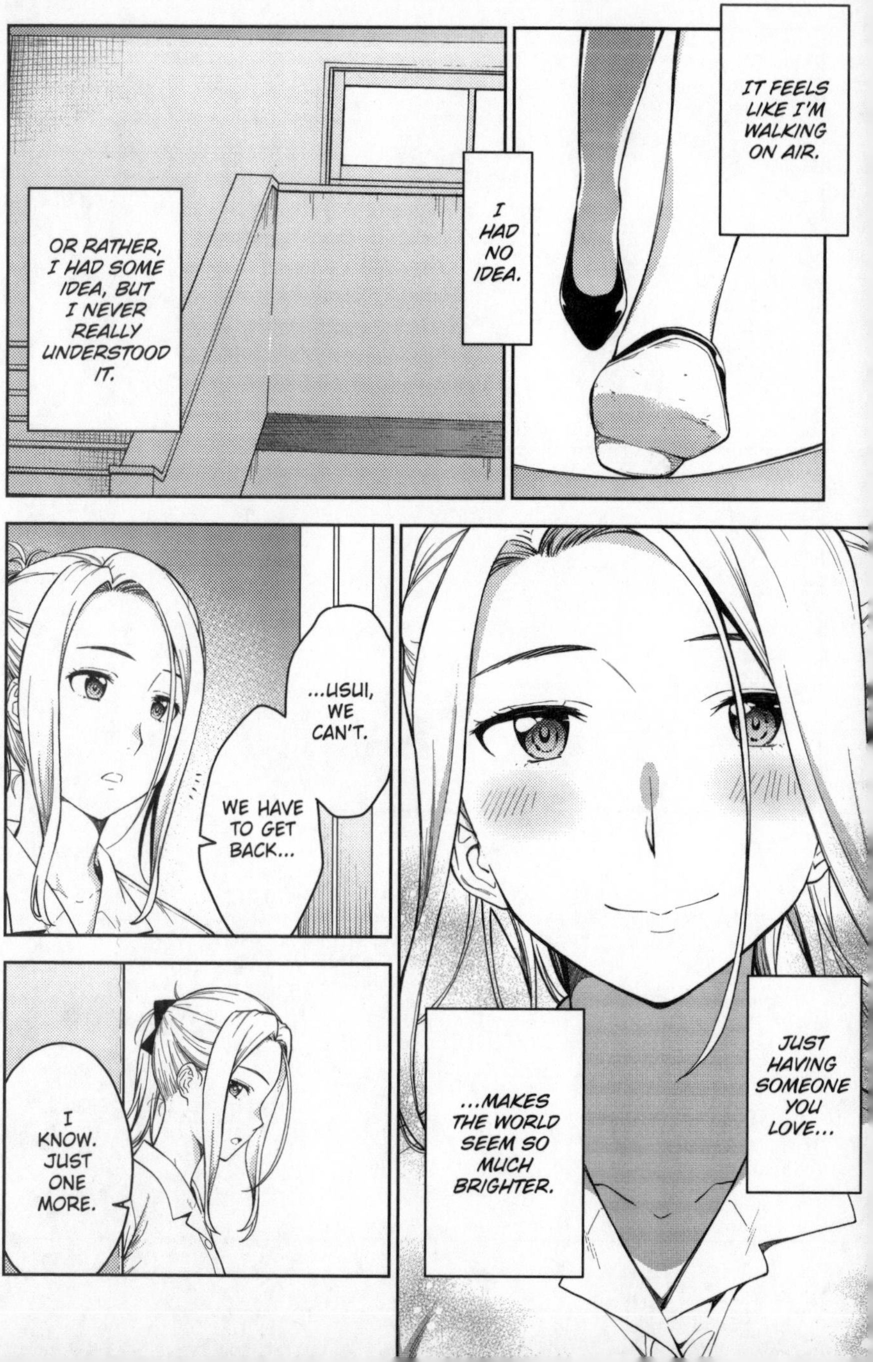
IT FEELS LIKE I'M WALKING ON AIR.
I HAD NO IDEA.
OR RATHER, I HAD SOME IDEA, BUT I NEVER REALLY UNDERSTOOD IT.
JUST HAVING SOMEONE YOU LOVE...
...MAKES THE WORLD SEEM SO MUCH BRIGHTER.
...USUI, WE CAN'T.
WE HAVE TO GET BACK...
I KNOW. JUST ONE MORE.

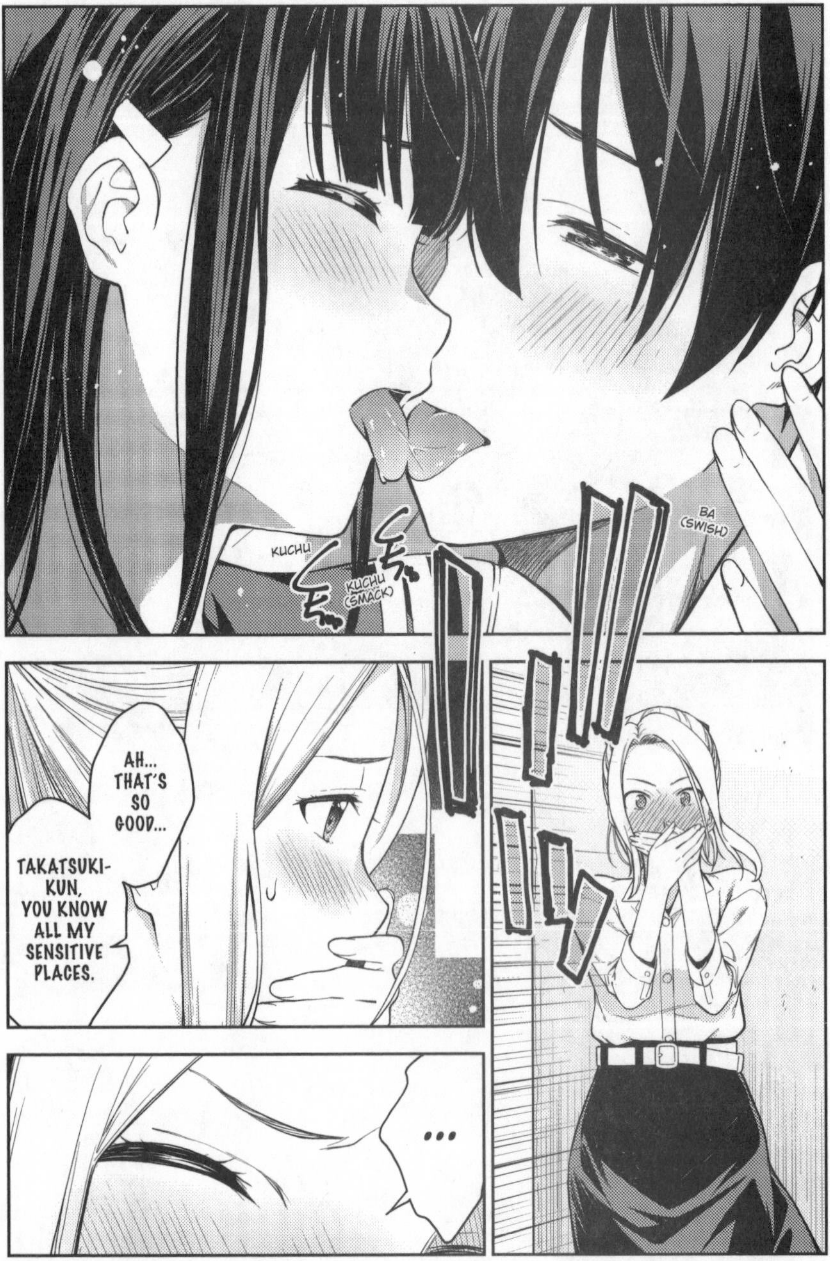
BA (SWISH)
KUCHU
KUCHU (SMACK)
AH... THAT'S SO GOOD...
TAKATSUKI-KUN, YOU KNOW ALL MY SENSITIVE PLACES.
...

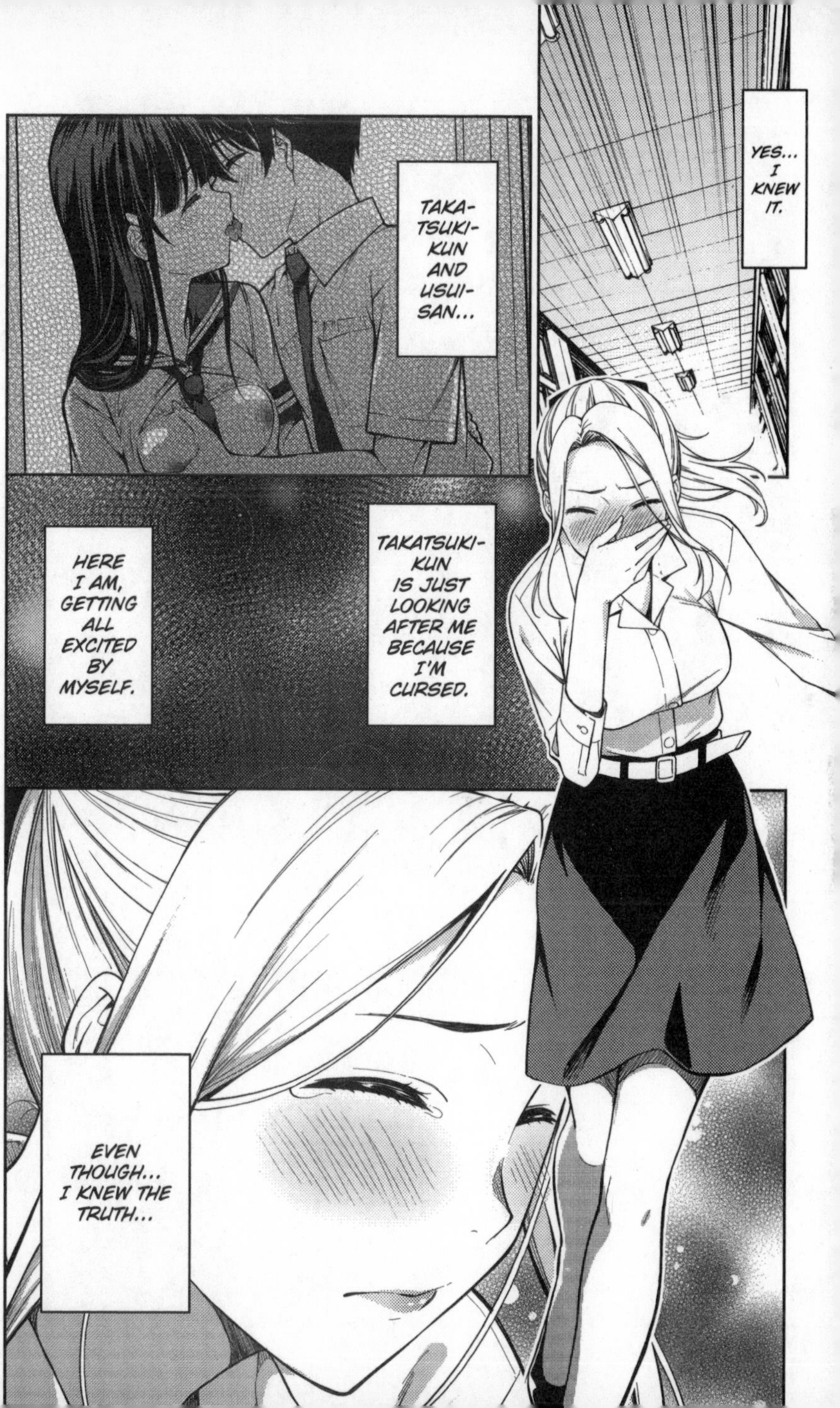
YES... I KNEW IT.
TAKA-TSUKI-KUN AND USUI-SAN...
TAKATSUKI-KUN IS JUST LOOKING AFTER ME BECAUSE I'M CURSED.
HERE I AM, GETTING ALL EXCITED BY MYSELF.
EVEN THOUGH... I KNEW THE TRUTH...

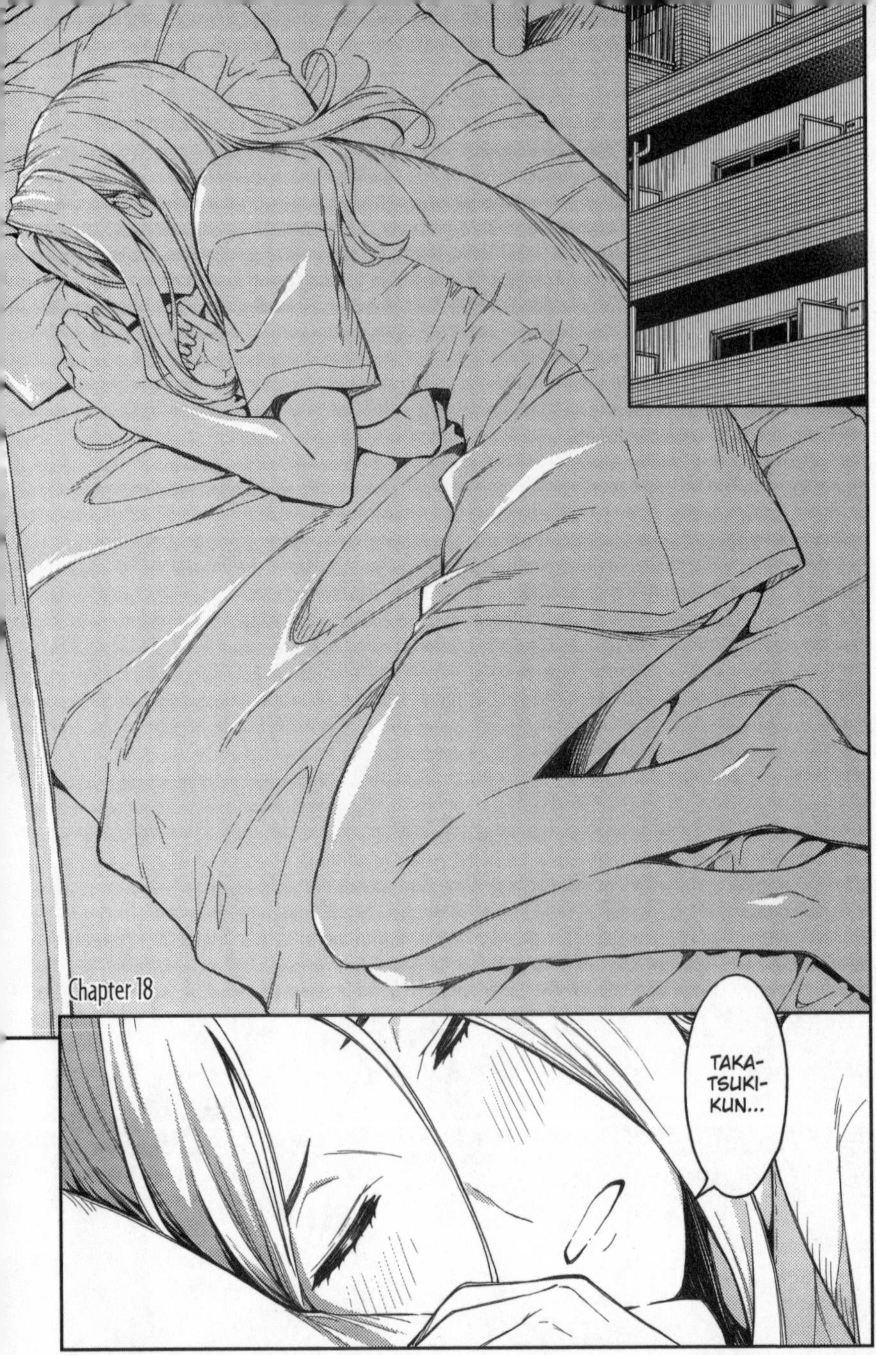
Chapter 18
TAKA-TSUKI-KUN...

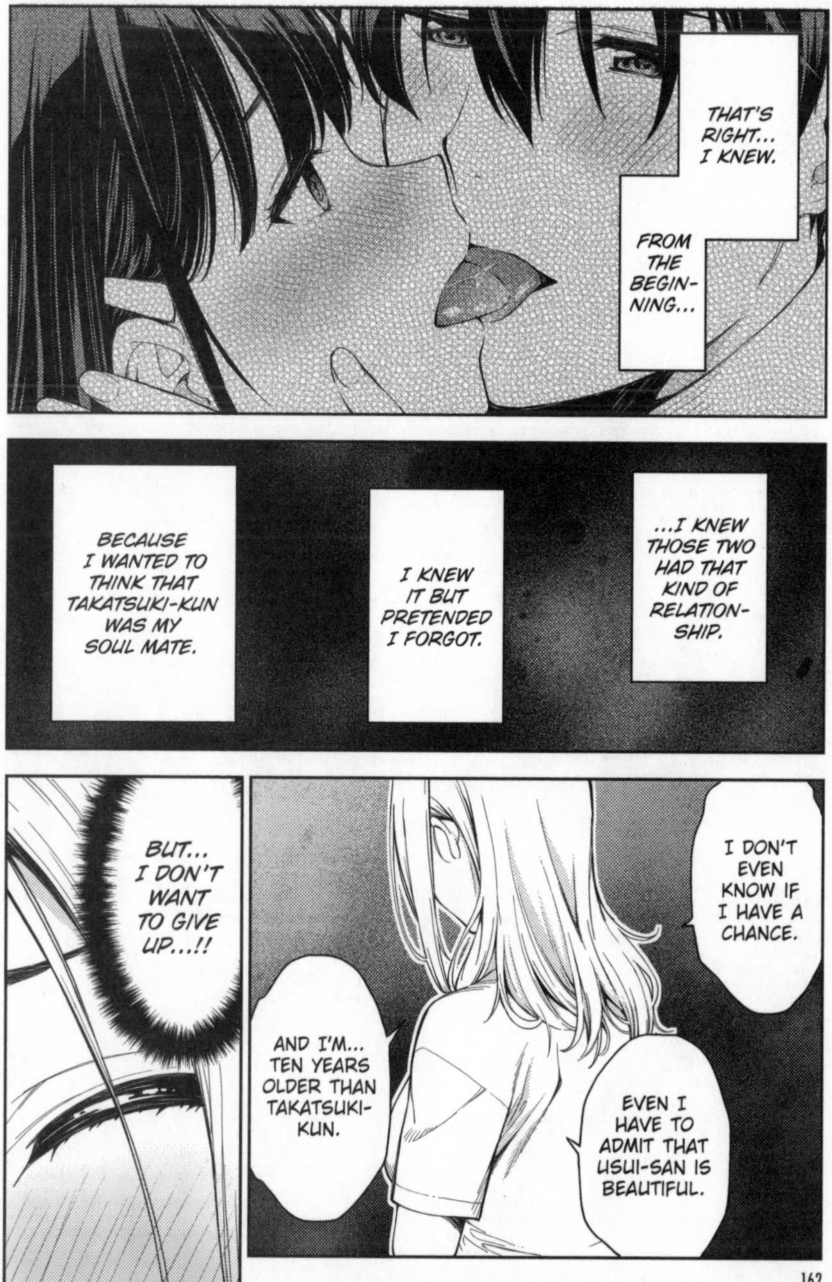
THAT'S RIGHT... I KNEW.
FROM THE BEGIN-NING...
...I KNEW THOSE TWO HAD THAT KIND OF RELATION-SHIP.
I KNEW IT BUT PRETENDED I FORGOT.
BECAUSE I WANTED TO THINK THAT TAKATSUKI-KUN WAS MY SOUL MATE.
I DON'T EVEN KNOW IF I HAVE A CHANCE.
AND I'M... TEN YEARS OLDER THAN TAKATSUKI-KUN.
EVEN I HAVE TO ADMIT THAT USUI-SAN IS BEAUTIFUL.
BUT... I DON'T WANT TO GIVE UP...!!

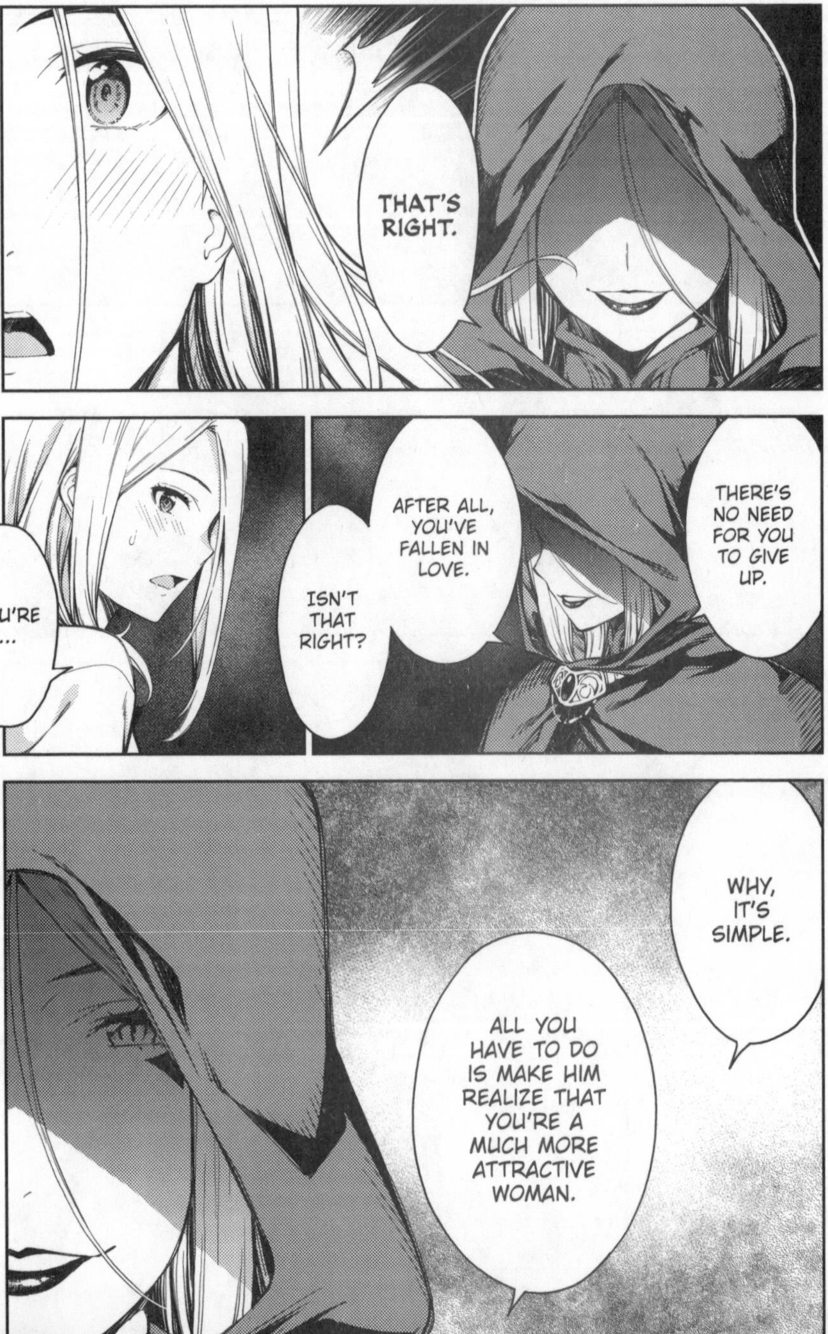
THAT'S RIGHT.
THERE'S NO NEED FOR YOU TO GIVE UP.
AFTER ALL, YOU'VE FALLEN IN LOVE.
ISN'T THAT RIGHT?
YOU'RE ...
WHY, IT'S SIMPLE.
ALL YOU HAVE TO DO IS MAKE HIM REALIZE THAT YOU'RE A MUCH MORE ATTRACTIVE WOMAN.

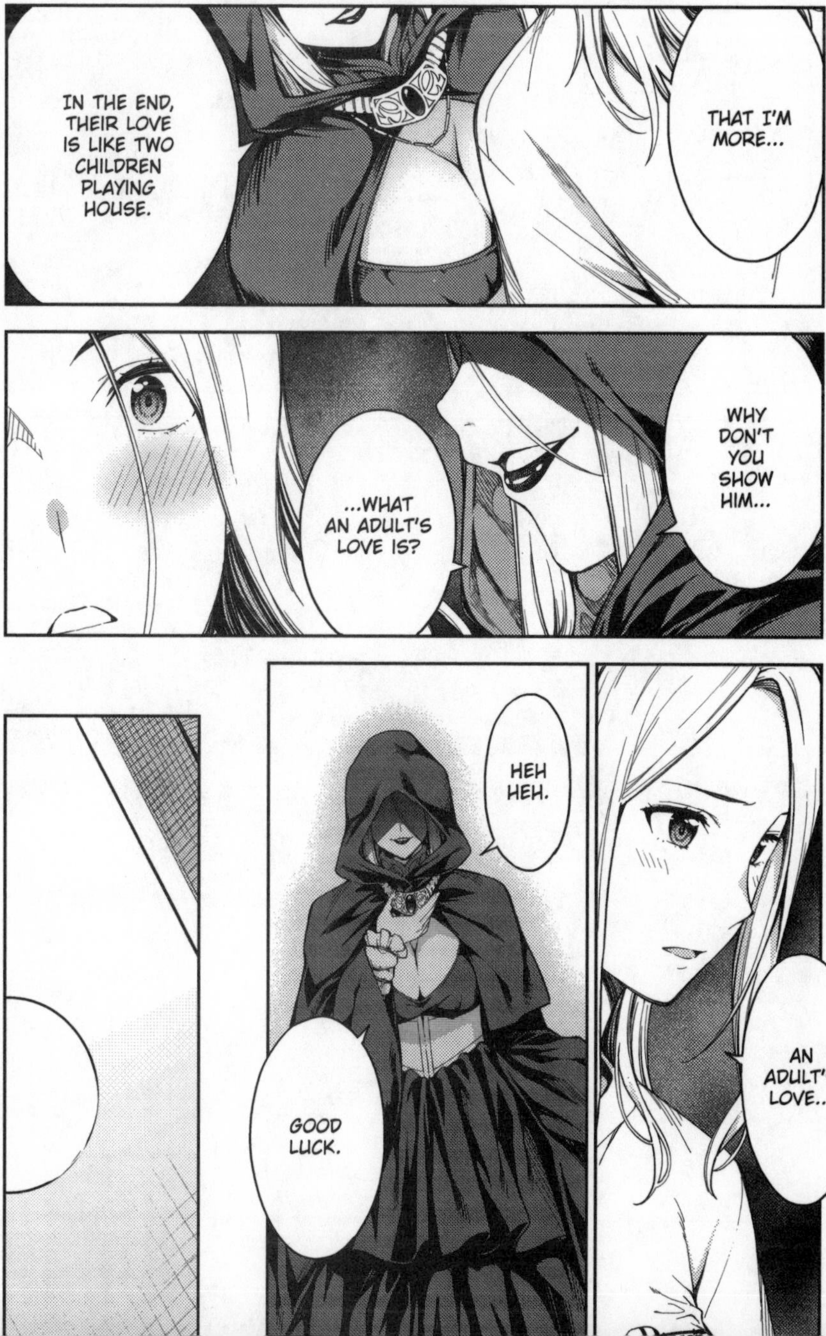
THAT I'M MORE...
IN THE END, THEIR LOVE IS LIKE TWO CHILDREN PLAYING HOUSE.
WHY DON'T YOU SHOW HIM...
...WHAT AN ADULT'S LOVE IS?
AN ADULT'S LOVE...
HEH HEH.
GOOD LUCK.

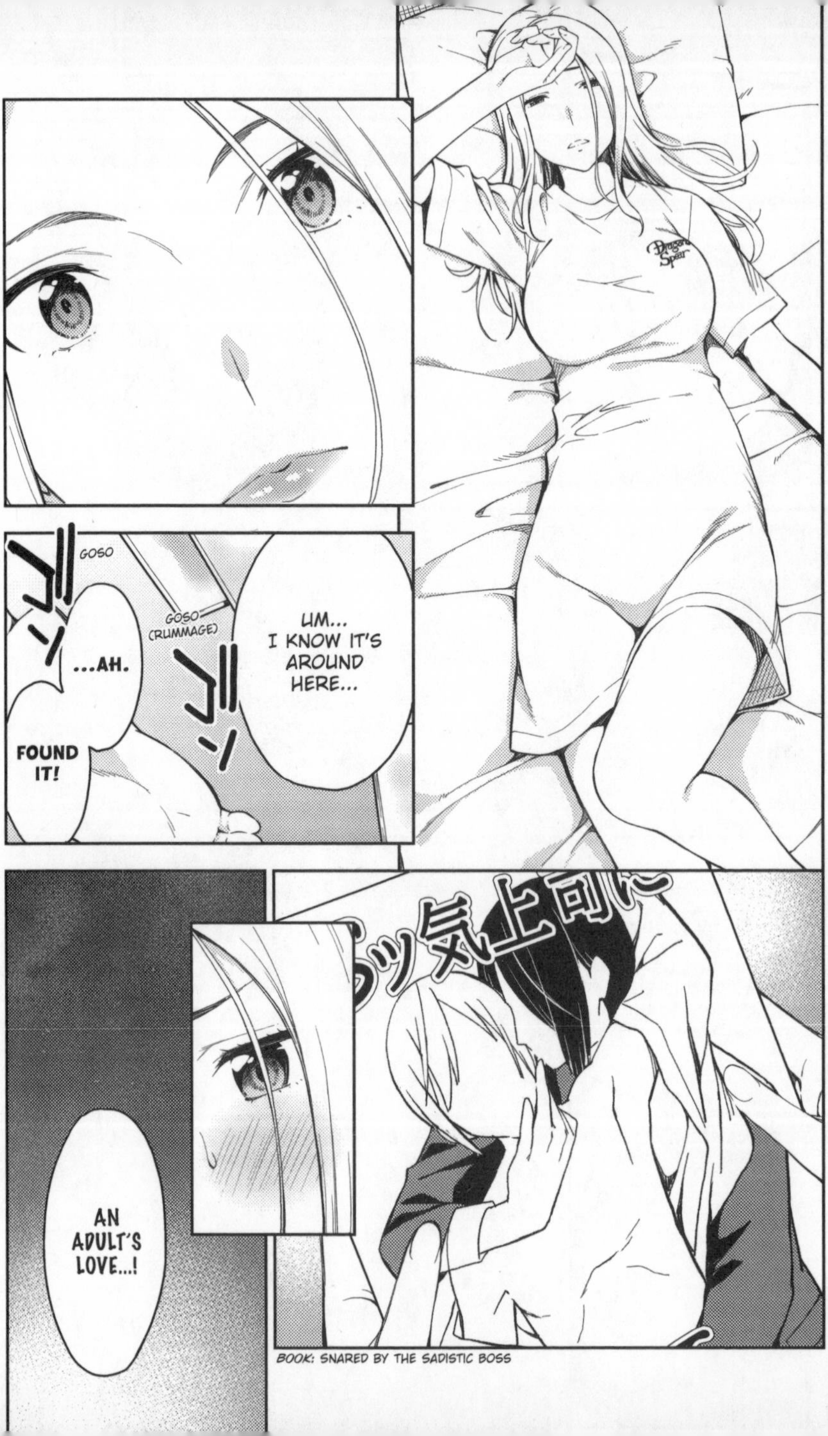

UM... I KNOW IT'S AROUND HERE...
GOSO (RUMMAGE)
GOSO
...AH.
FOUND IT!
ッ気上司に
AN ADULT'S LOVE...!
BOOK: SNARED BY THE SADISTIC BOSS

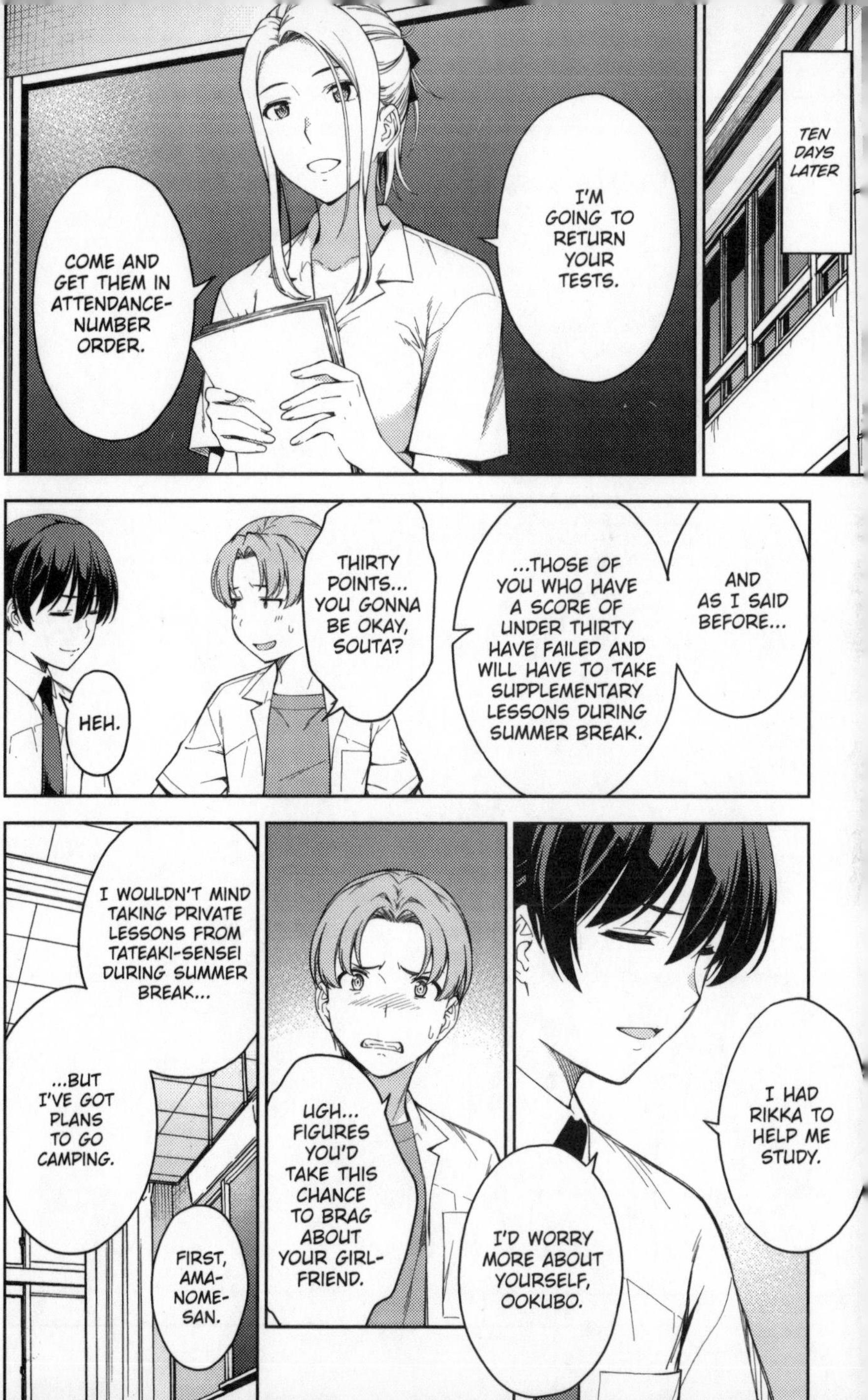
TEN DAYS LATER
I'M GOING TO RETURN YOUR TESTS.
COME AND GET THEM IN ATTENDANCE-NUMBER ORDER.
AND AS I SAID BEFORE...
...THOSE OF YOU WHO HAVE A SCORE OF UNDER THIRTY HAVE FAILED AND WILL HAVE TO TAKE SUPPLEMENTARY LESSONS DURING SUMMER BREAK.
THIRTY POINTS... YOU GONNA BE OKAY, SOUTA?
HEH.
I HAD RIKKA TO HELP ME STUDY.
I'D WORRY MORE ABOUT YOURSELF, OOKUBO.
UGH... FIGURES YOU'D TAKE THIS CHANCE TO BRAG ABOUT YOUR GIRL-FRIEND.
I WOULDN'T MIND TAKING PRIVATE LESSONS FROM TATEAKI-SENSEI DURING SUMMER BREAK...
...BUT I'VE GOT PLANS TO GO CAMPING.
FIRST, AMA-NOME-SAN.

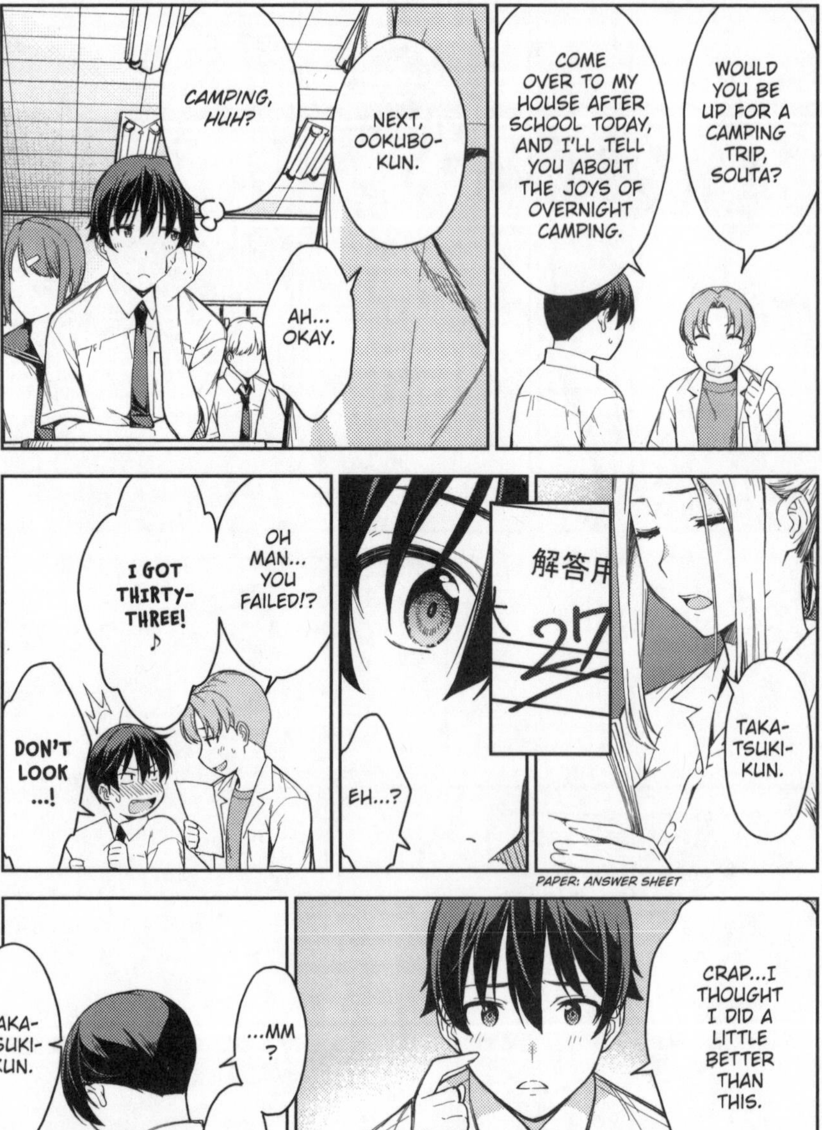
WOULD YOU BE UP FOR A CAMPING TRIP, SOUTA?
COME OVER TO MY HOUSE AFTER SCHOOL TODAY, AND I'LL TELL YOU ABOUT THE JOYS OF OVERNIGHT CAMPING.
NEXT, OOKUBO-KUN.
CAMPING, HUH?
AH... OKAY.
TAKA-TSUKI-KUN.
解答用
27
EH...?
PAPER: ANSWER SHEET
OH MAN... YOU FAILED!?
I GOT THIRTY-THREE! ♪
DON'T LOOK ...!
CRAP...I THOUGHT I DID A LITTLE BETTER THAN THIS.
TAKA-TSUKI-KUN.
...MM ?
HUH ...?

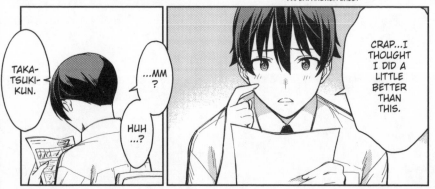

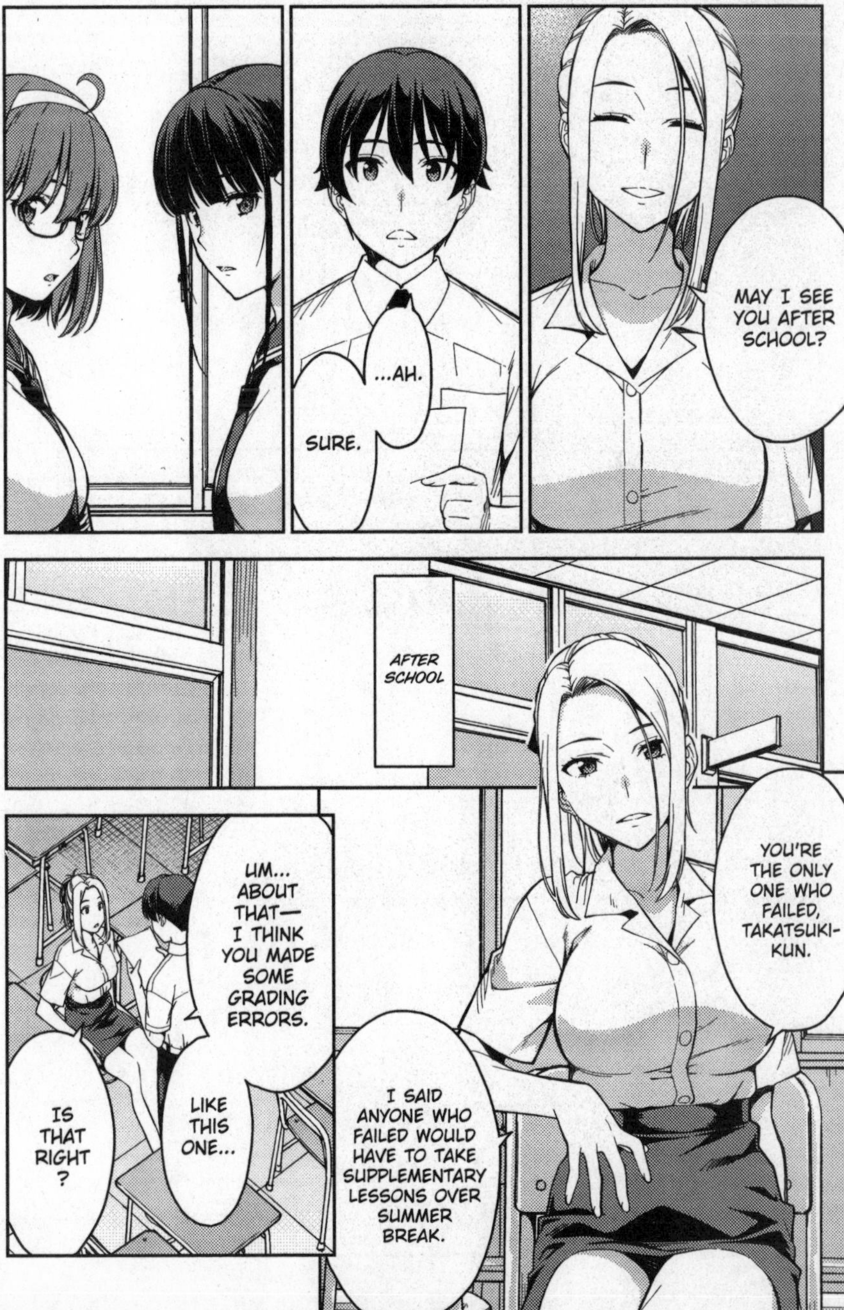
MAY I SEE YOU AFTER SCHOOL?
...AH.
SURE.
AFTER SCHOOL
YOU'RE THE ONLY ONE WHO FAILED, TAKATSUKI-KUN.
I SAID ANYONE WHO FAILED WOULD HAVE TO TAKE SUPPLEMENTARY LESSONS OVER SUMMER BREAK.
UM... ABOUT THAT— I THINK YOU MADE SOME GRADING ERRORS.
LIKE THIS ONE...
IS THAT RIGHT?

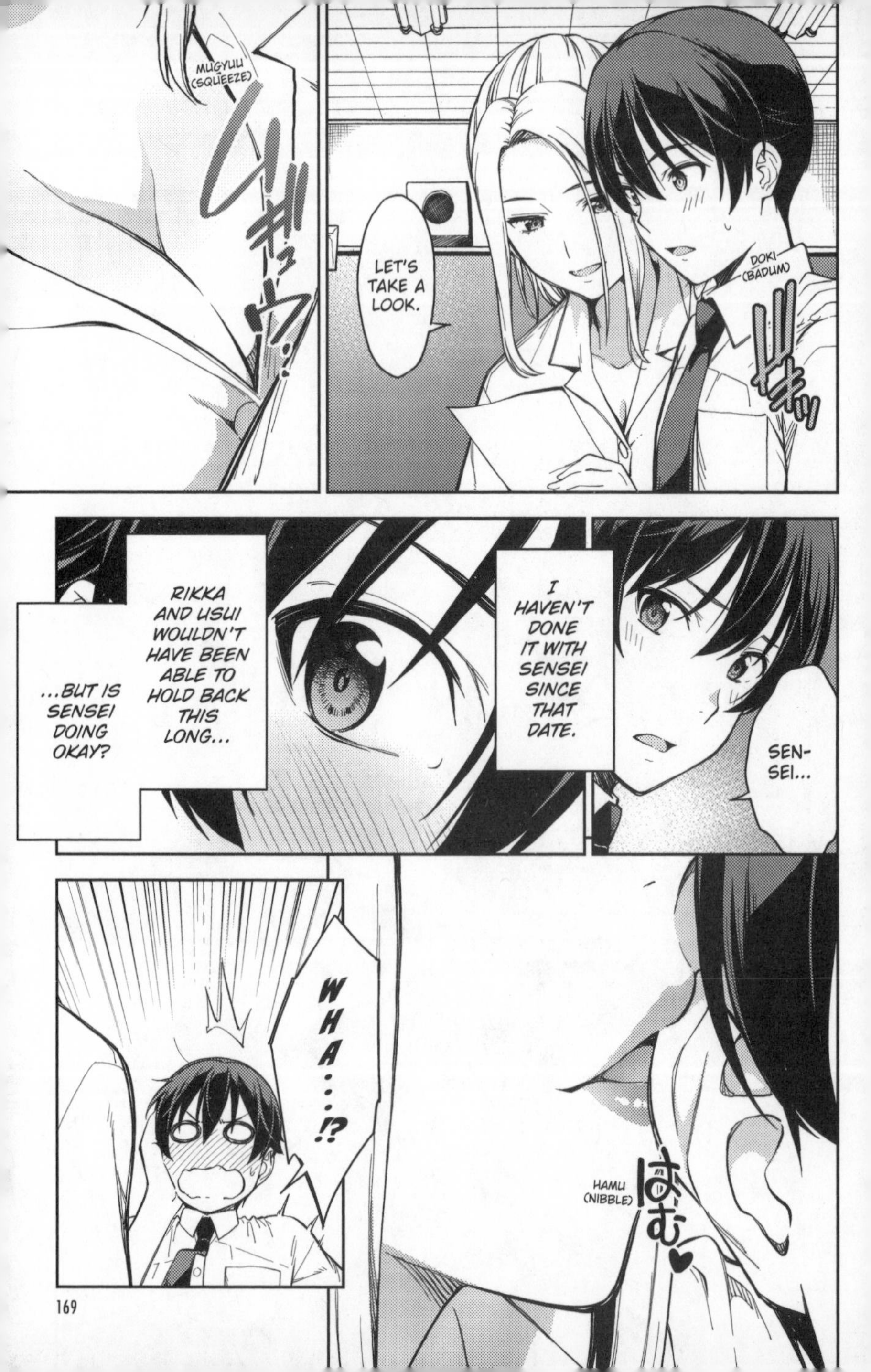
LET'S TAKE A LOOK.
DOKI (BADUM)
MUGYUU (SQUEEZE)
SEN-SEI...
I HAVEN'T DONE IT WITH SENSEI SINCE THAT DATE.
RIKKA AND USUI WOULDN'T HAVE BEEN ABLE TO HOLD BACK THIS LONG...
...BUT IS SENSEI DOING OKAY?
HAMU (NIBBLE)
はむ♥
WHA...!?

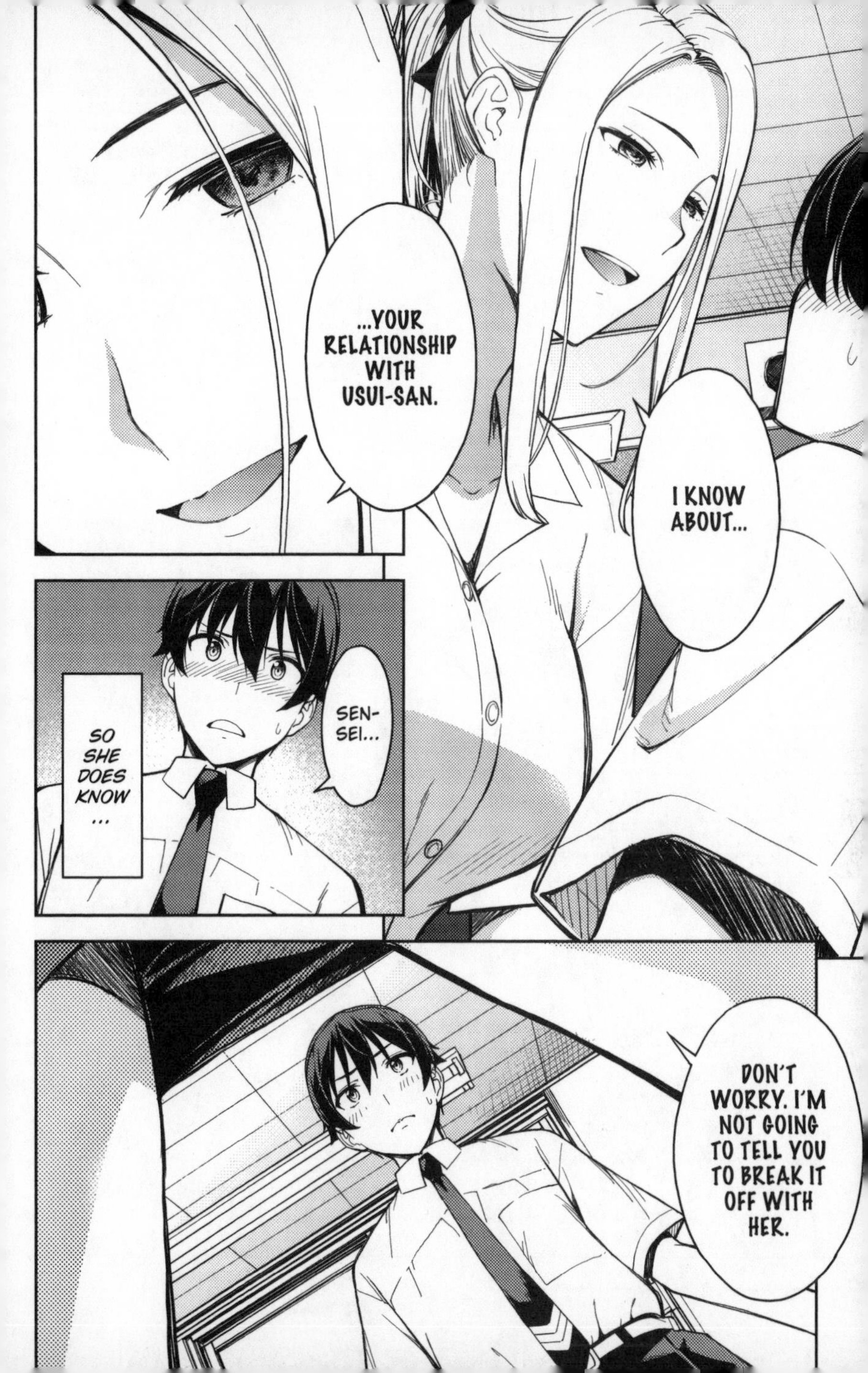
I KNOW ABOUT...
...YOUR RELATIONSHIP WITH USUI-SAN.
SEN-SEI...
SO SHE DOES KNOW...
DON'T WORRY. I'M NOT GOING TO TELL YOU TO BREAK IT OFF WITH HER.

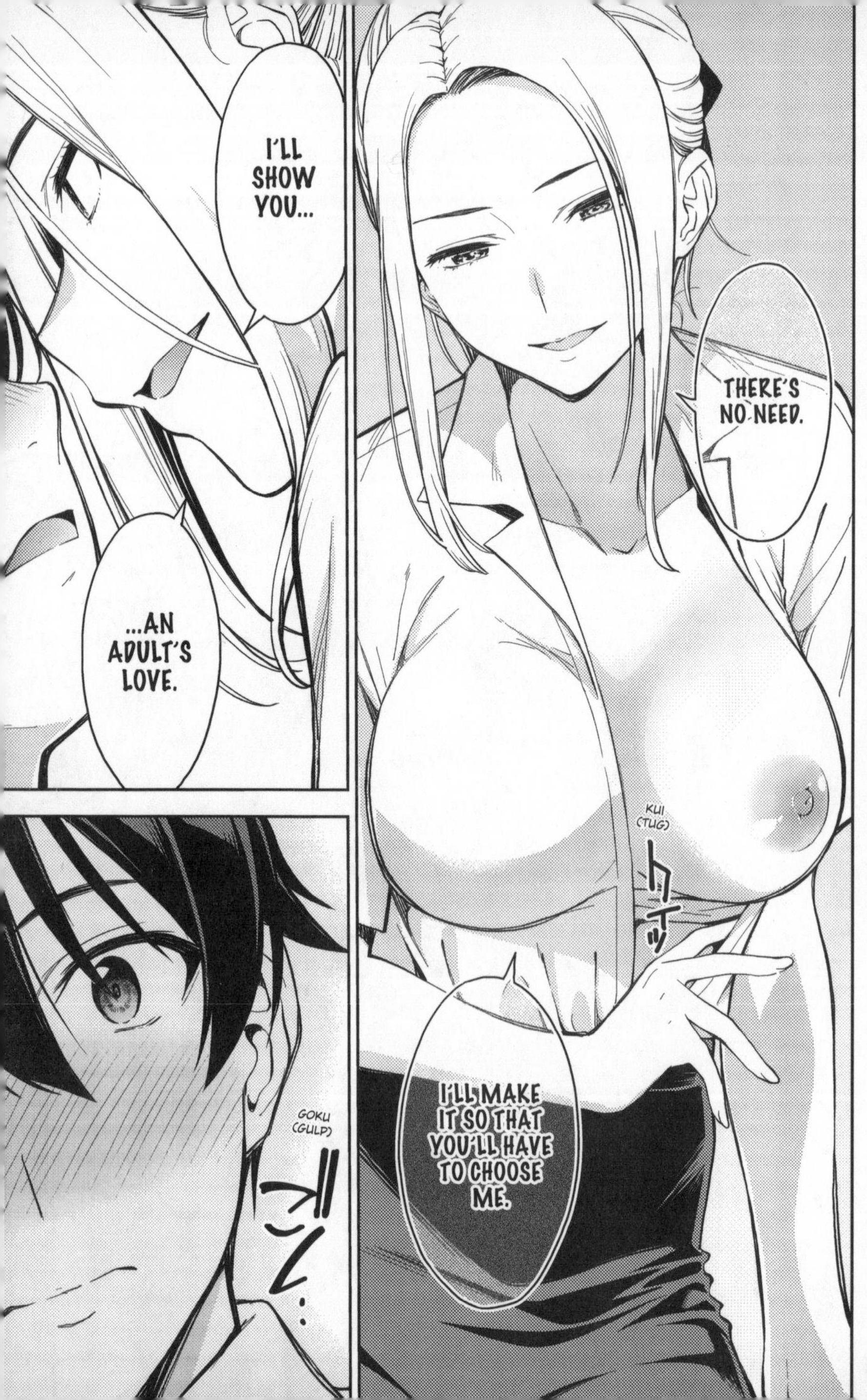
THERE'S NO NEED.
KUI (TUG)
I'LL MAKE IT SO THAT YOU'LL HAVE TO CHOOSE ME.
I'LL SHOW YOU...
...AN ADULT'S LOVE.
GOKU (GULP)

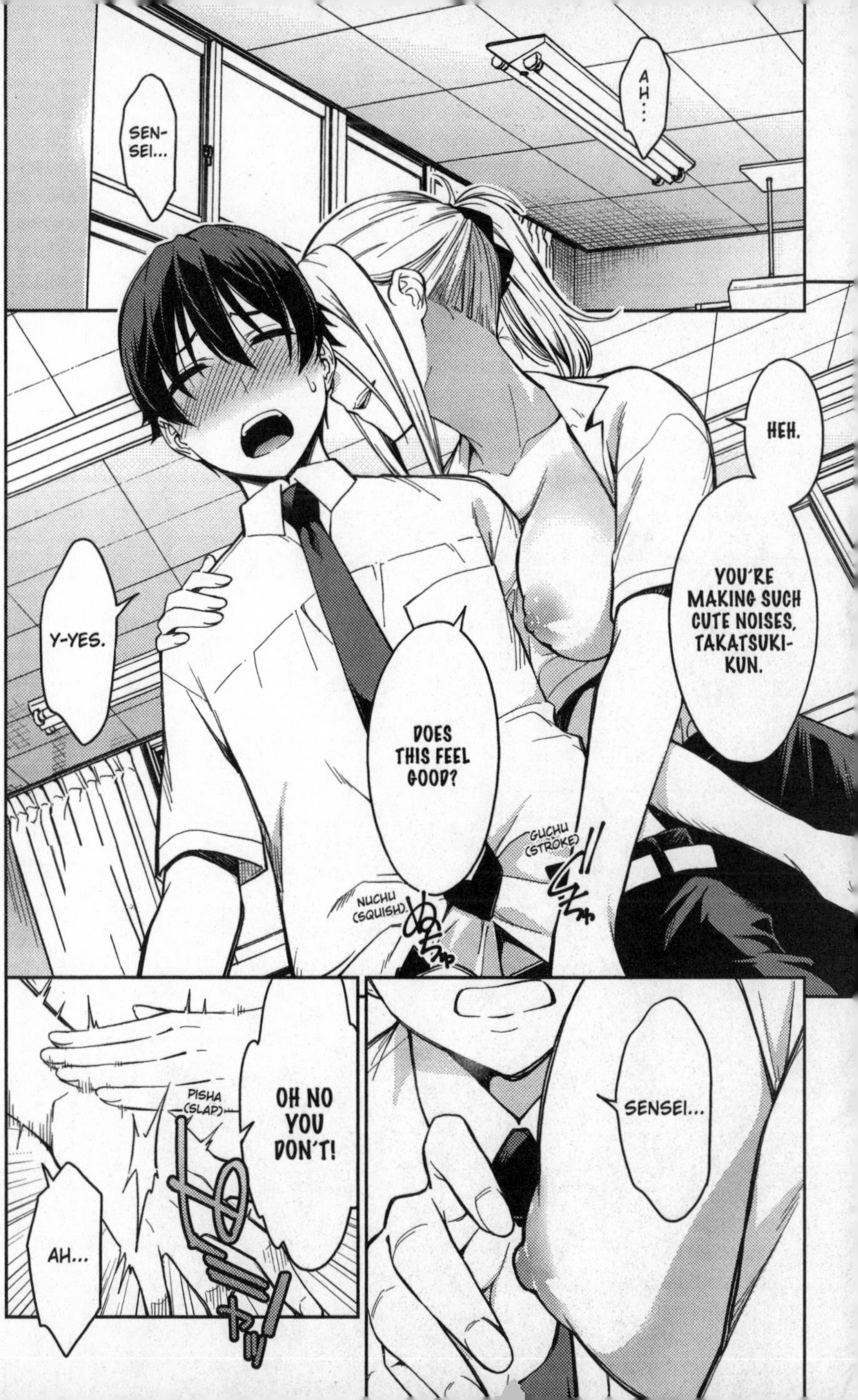
AH...
SEN-SEI...
HEH.
YOU'RE MAKING SUCH CUTE NOISES, TAKATSUKI-KUN.
DOES THIS FEEL GOOD?
GUCHU (STROKE)
NUCHU (SQUISH)
Y-YES.
SENSEI...
OH NO YOU DON'T!
PISHA (SLAP)
AH...

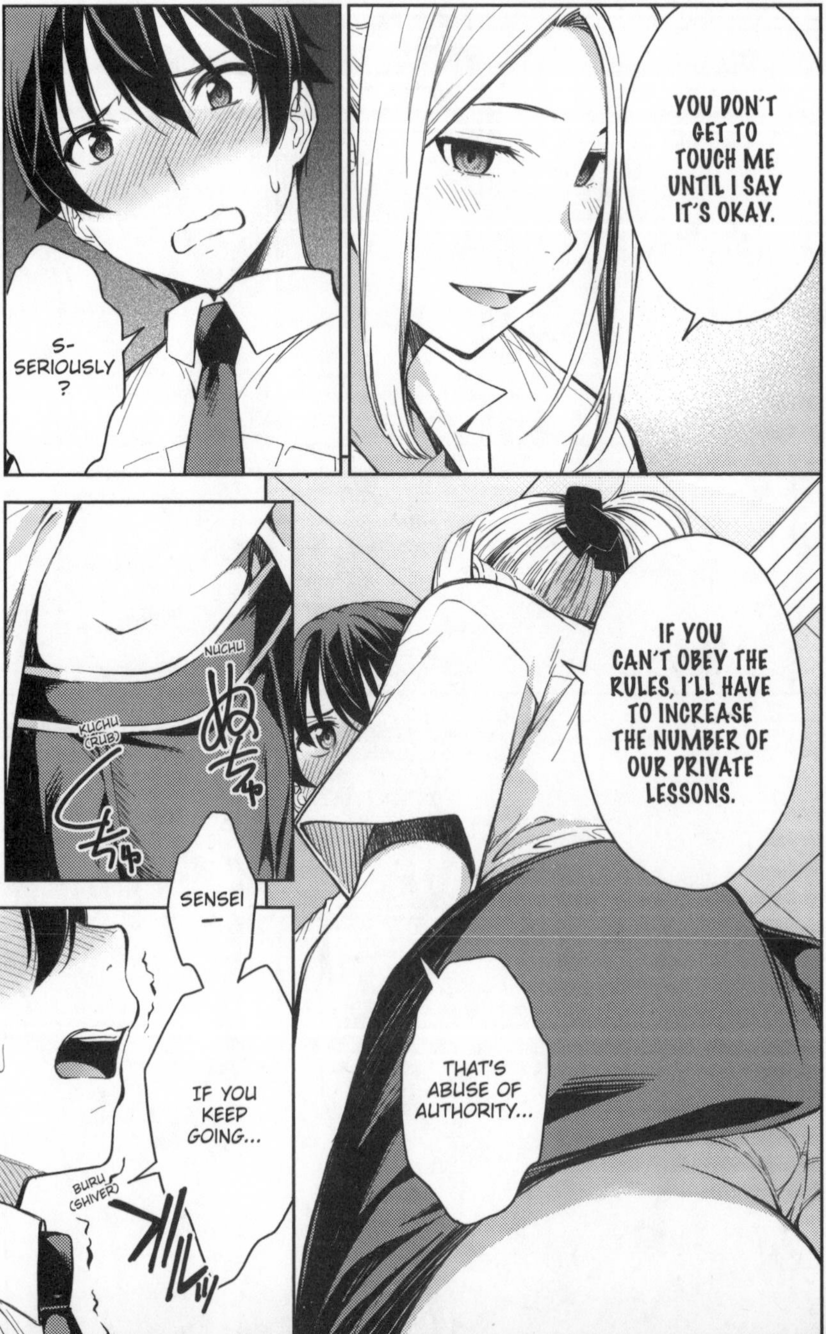
YOU DON'T GET TO TOUCH ME UNTIL I SAY IT'S OKAY.
S-SERIOUSLY?
IF YOU CAN'T OBEY THE RULES, I'LL HAVE TO INCREASE THE NUMBER OF OUR PRIVATE LESSONS.
NUCHU
KUCHU (RUB)
SENSEI—
THAT'S ABUSE OF AUTHORITY...
IF YOU KEEP GOING...
BURU (SHIVER)

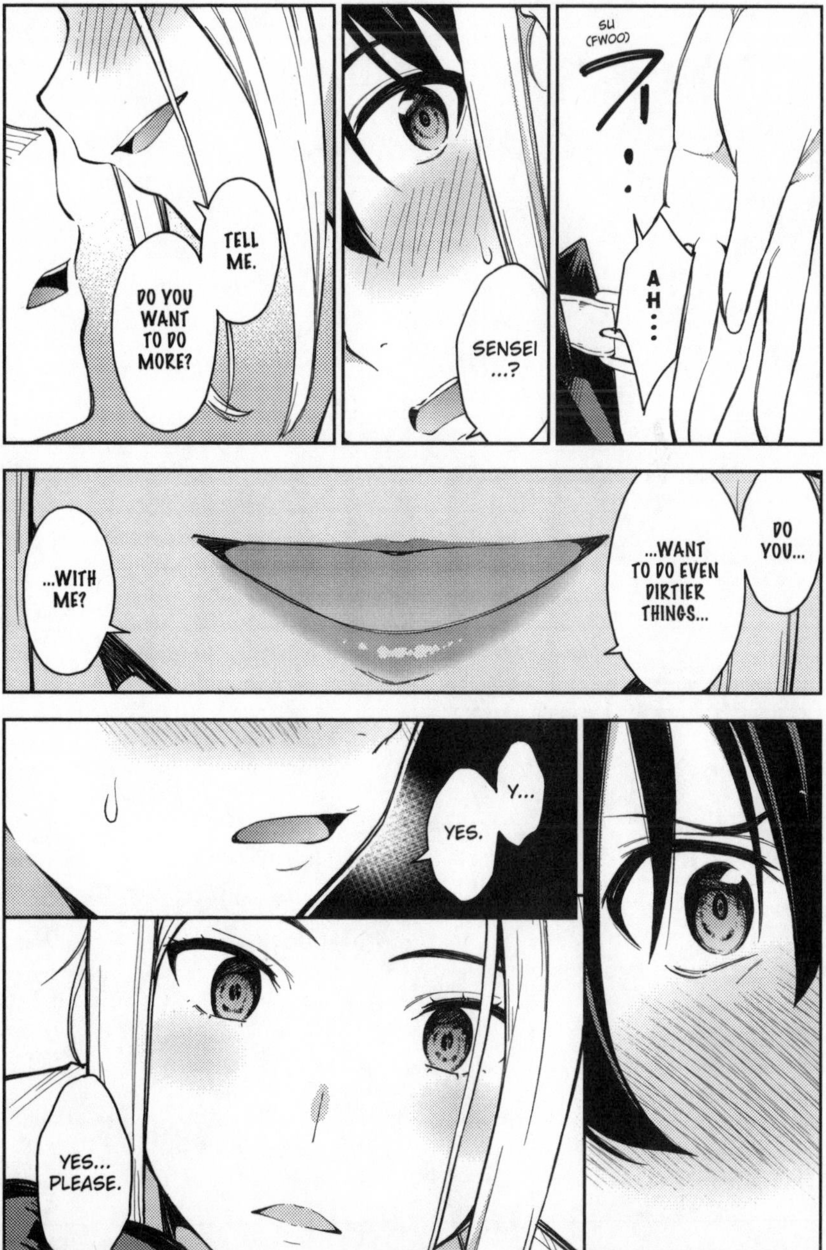
SU (FWOO)
AH...
SENSEI ...?
TELL ME.
DO YOU WANT TO DO MORE?
DO YOU...
...WANT TO DO EVEN DIRTIER THINGS...
...WITH ME?
Y... YES.
YES... PLEASE.

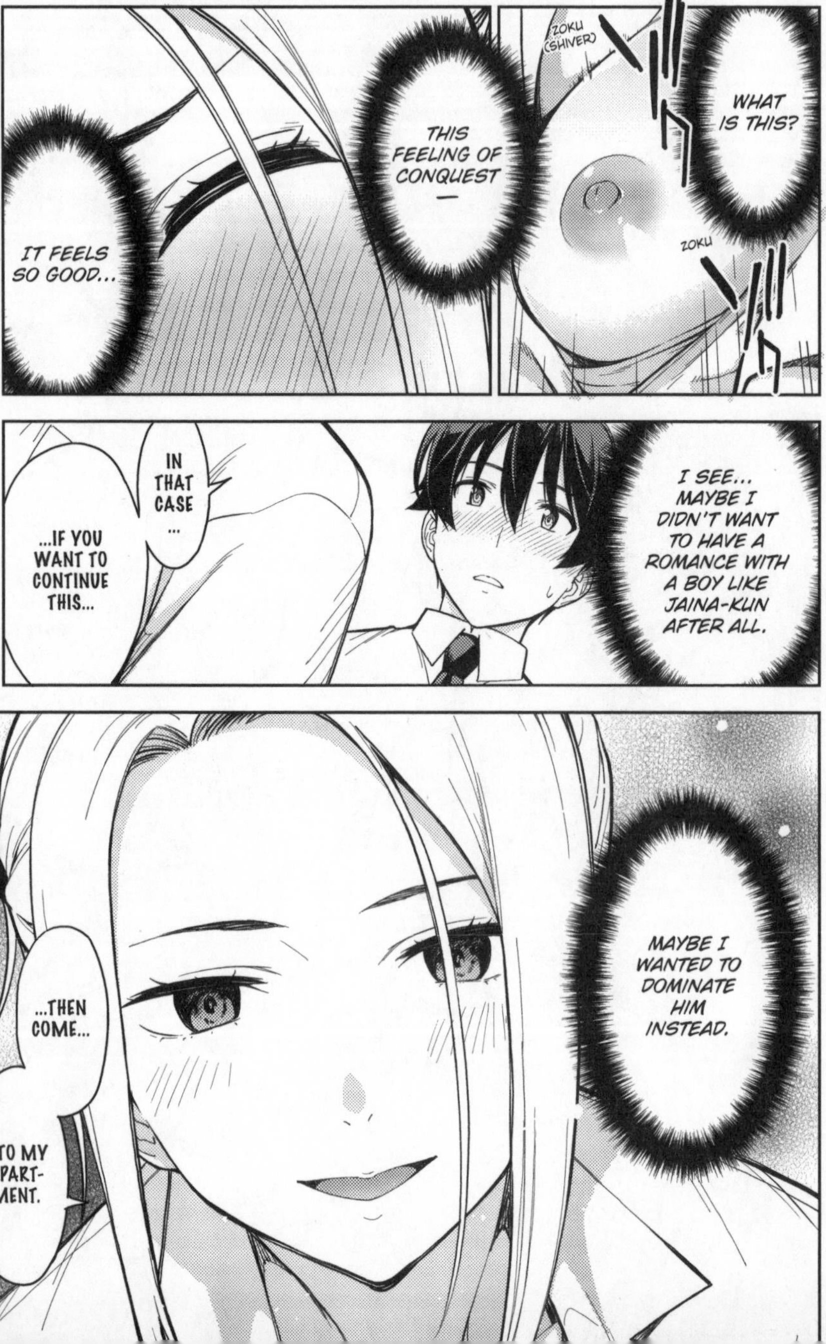
ZOKU (SHIVER)
WHAT IS THIS?
ZOKU
THIS FEELING OF CONQUEST —
IT FEELS SO GOOD...
I SEE... MAYBE I DIDN'T WANT TO HAVE A ROMANCE WITH A BOY LIKE JAINA-KUN AFTER ALL.
IN THAT CASE...
...IF YOU WANT TO CONTINUE THIS...
MAYBE I WANTED TO DOMINATE HIM INSTEAD.
...THEN COME...
...TO MY APARTMENT.

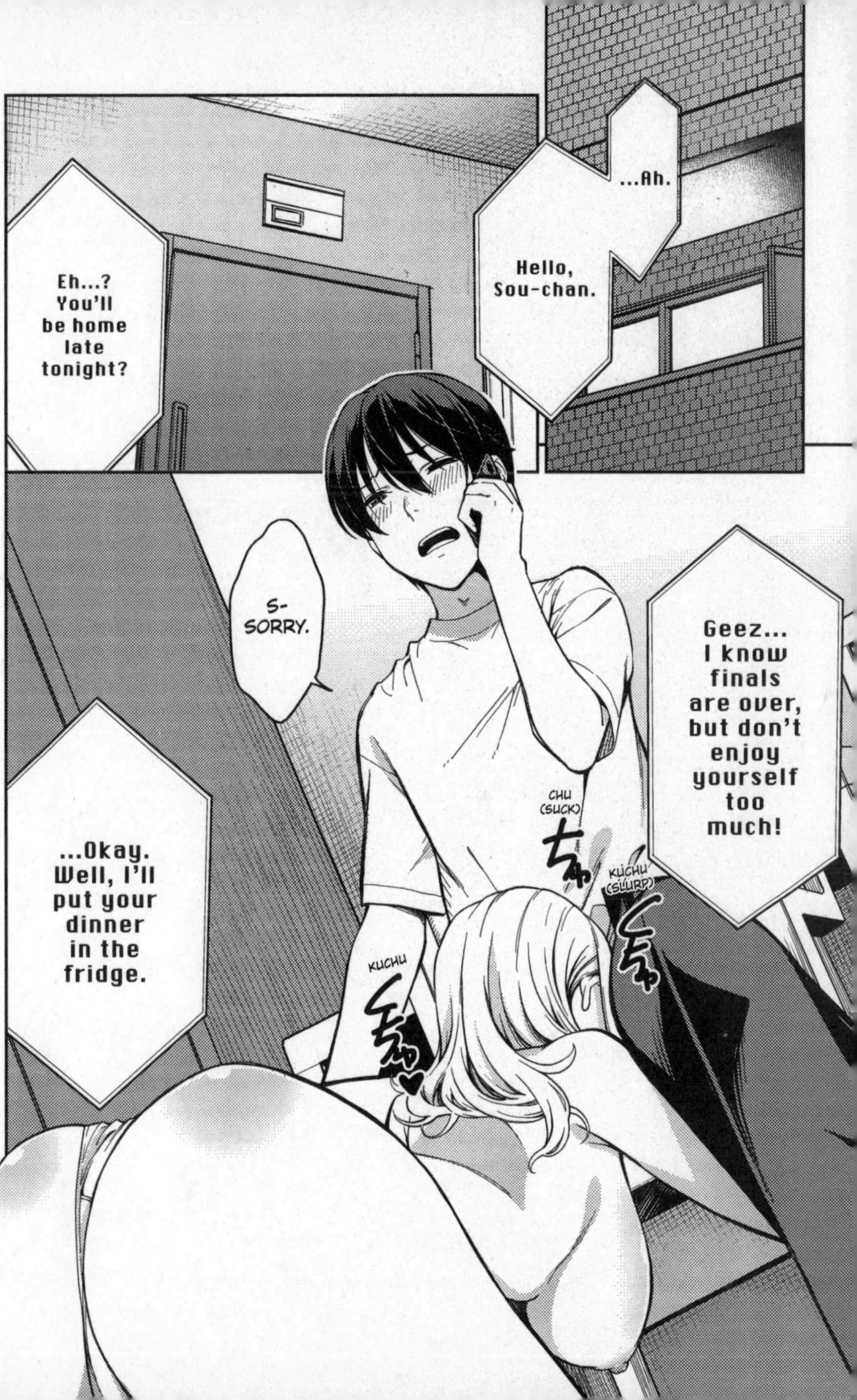
...Ah.
Hello, Sou-chan.
Eh...? You'll be home late tonight?
Geez... I know finals are over, but don't enjoy yourself too much!
S-SORRY.
CHU (SUCK)
KUCHU (SLURP)
KUCHU
...Okay. Well, I'll put your dinner in the fridge.

RERO
(LICK)

And don't be home too late, Sou-chan.

AH...!!

I—I WON'T.

DON'T HOLD BACK.

YOU CAN CRY OUT MORE THAN THAT.

What's wrong? You made a weird noise.

I-IT WAS NOTHING.

...Huh? Is someone with you?

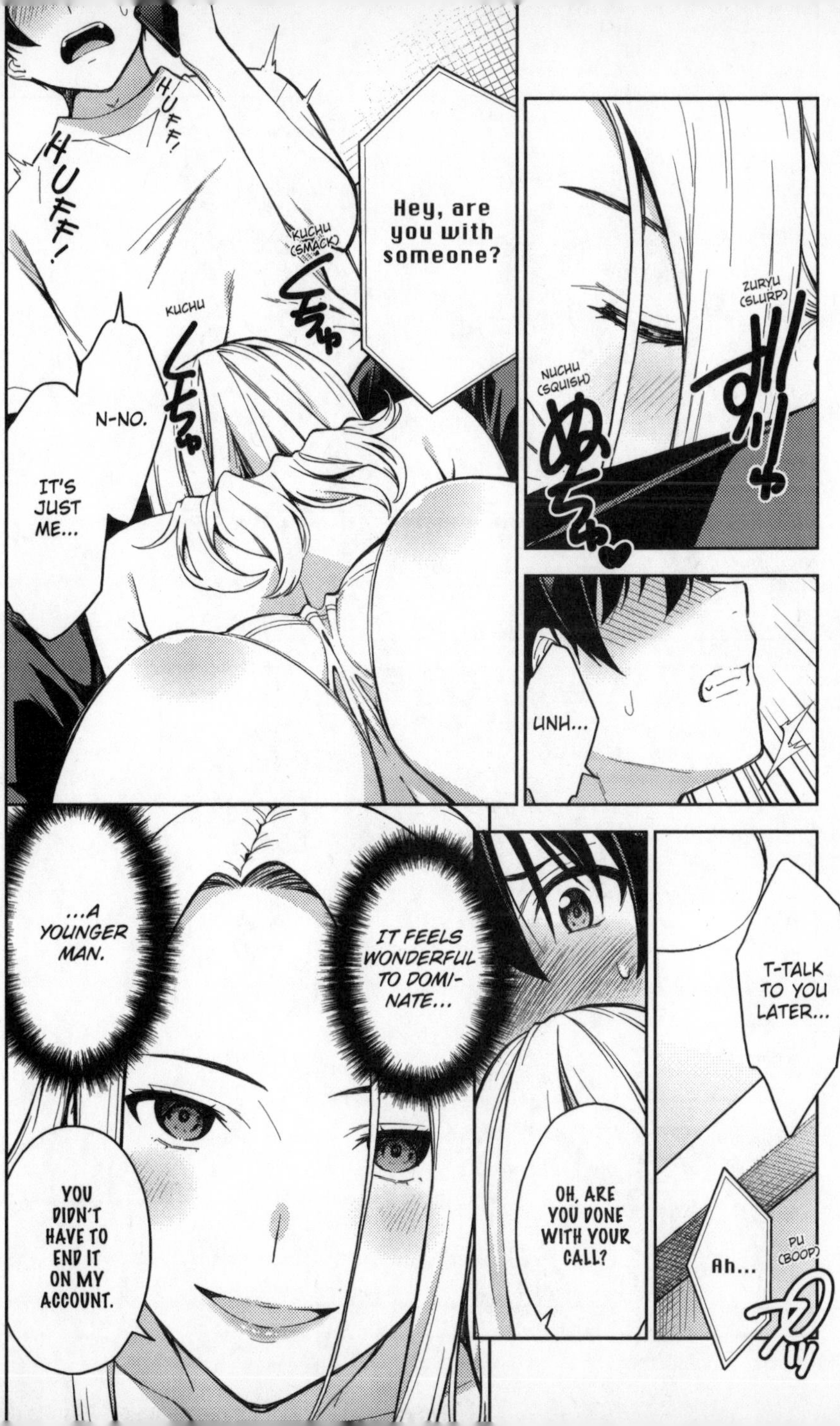
ZURYU (SLURP)
NUCHU (SQUISH)
UNH...
Hey, are you with someone?
HUFF! HUFF!
KUCHU (SMACK)
KUCHU
N-NO.
IT'S JUST ME...
T-TALK TO YOU LATER...
Ah...
PU (BOOP)
OH, ARE YOU DONE WITH YOUR CALL?
IT FEELS WONDERFUL TO DOMI-NATE...
...A YOUNGER MAN.
YOU DIDN'T HAVE TO END IT ON MY ACCOUNT.

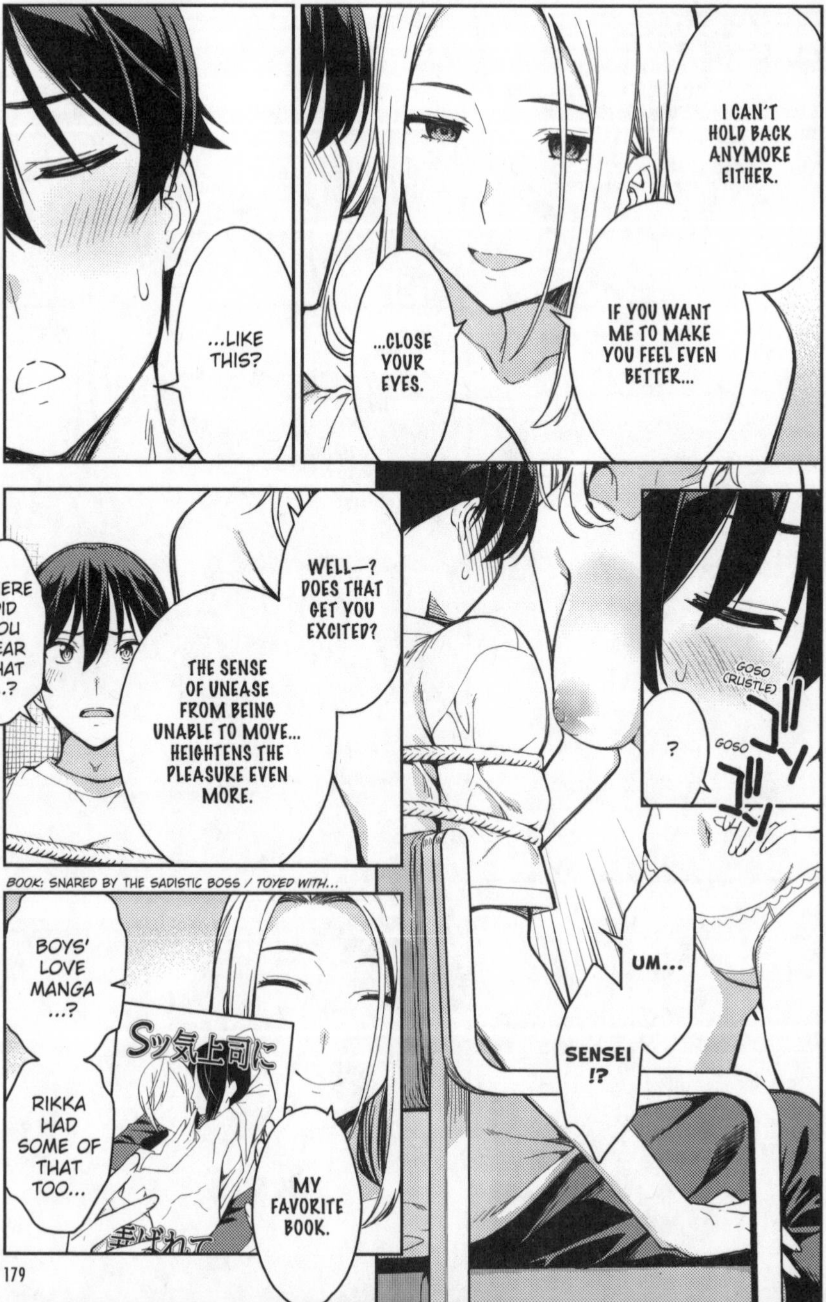
I CAN'T HOLD BACK ANYMORE EITHER.
IF YOU WANT ME TO MAKE YOU FEEL EVEN BETTER...
...CLOSE YOUR EYES.
...LIKE THIS?
GOSO (RUSTLE)
GOSO
?
UM...
SENSEI!?
WELL—? DOES THAT GET YOU EXCITED?
THE SENSE OF UNEASE FROM BEING UNABLE TO MOVE... HEIGHTENS THE PLEASURE EVEN MORE.
WHERE DID YOU HEAR THAT...?
BOOK: SNARED BY THE SADISTIC BOSS / TOYED WITH...
Sッ気上司に
MY FAVORITE BOOK.
BOYS' LOVE MANGA...?
RIKKA HAD SOME OF THAT TOO...

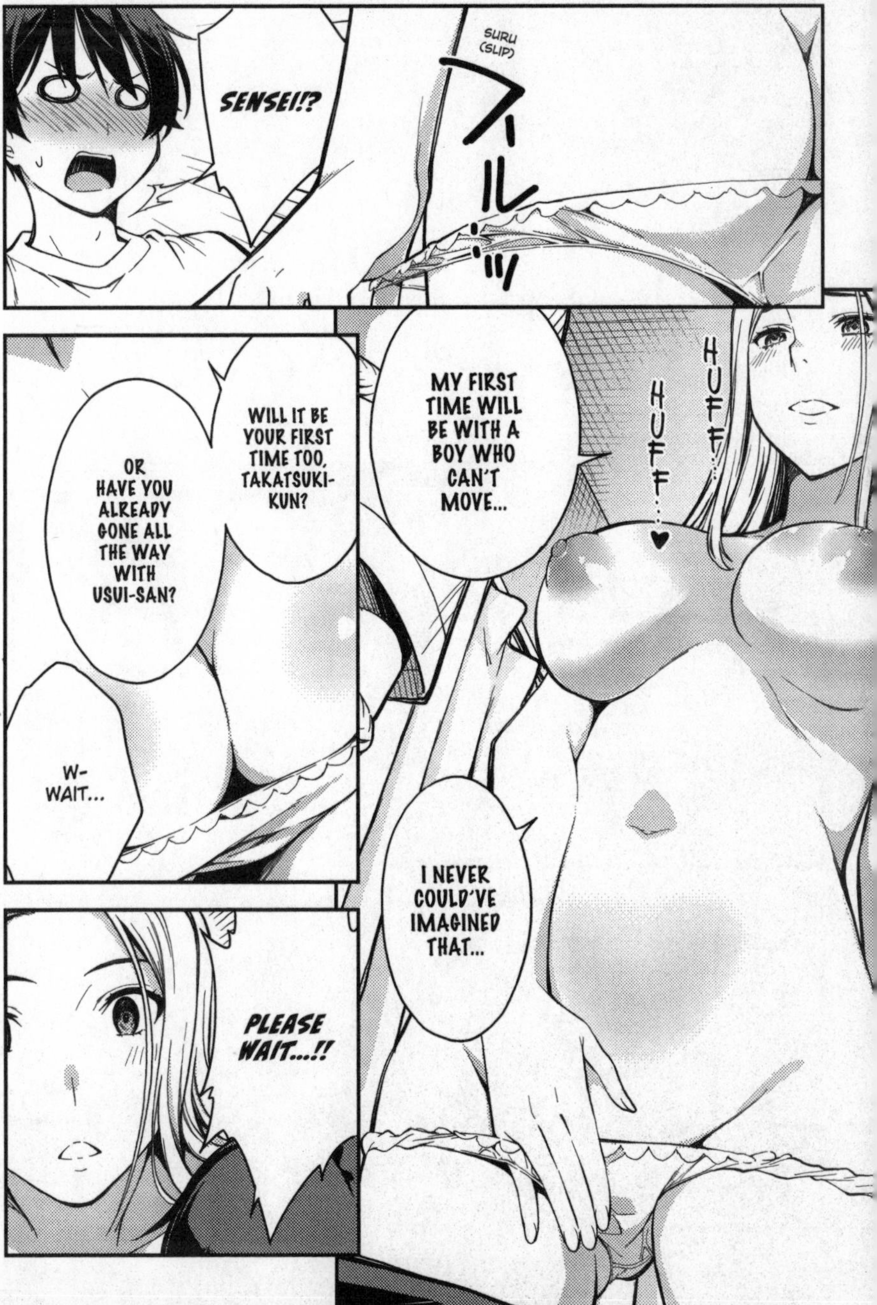

SURU (SLIP)
スルッ
SENSEI!?
HUFF HUFF...♥
MY FIRST TIME WILL BE WITH A BOY WHO CAN'T MOVE...
I NEVER COULD'VE IMAGINED THAT...
WILL IT BE YOUR FIRST TIME TOO, TAKATSUKI-KUN?
OR HAVE YOU ALREADY GONE ALL THE WAY WITH USUI-SAN?
W-WAIT...
PLEASE WAIT...!!

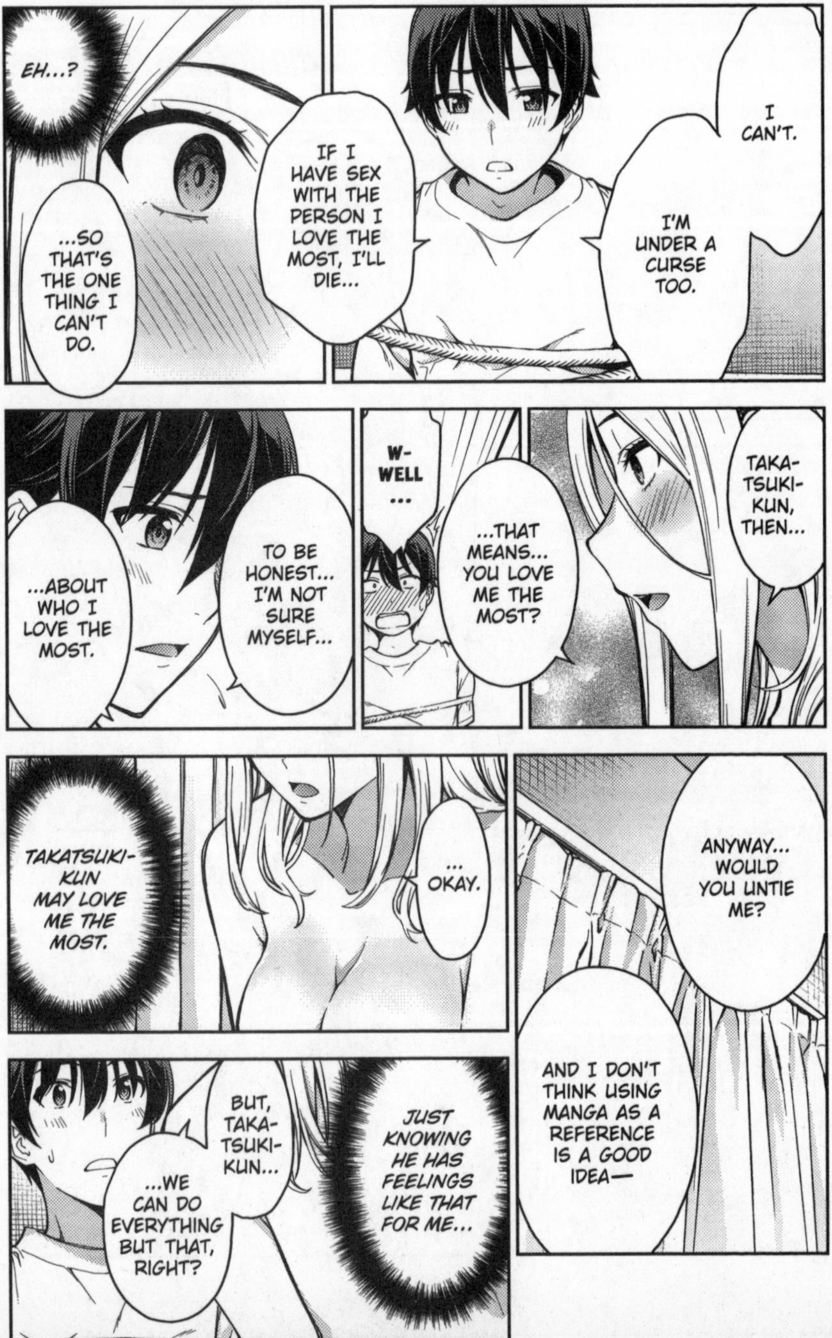
I CAN'T.
I'M UNDER A CURSE TOO.
IF I HAVE SEX WITH THE PERSON I LOVE THE MOST, I'LL DIE...
EH...?
...SO THAT'S THE ONE THING I CAN'T DO.
TAKA-TSUKI-KUN, THEN...
...THAT MEANS... YOU LOVE ME THE MOST?
W-WELL...
TO BE HONEST... I'M NOT SURE MYSELF...
...ABOUT WHO I LOVE THE MOST.
ANYWAY... WOULD YOU UNTIE ME?
AND I DON'T THINK USING MANGA AS A REFERENCE IS A GOOD IDEA—
...OKAY.
TAKATSUKI-KUN MAY LOVE ME THE MOST.
JUST KNOWING HE HAS FEELINGS LIKE THAT FOR ME...
BUT, TAKA-TSUKI-KUN...
...WE CAN DO EVERYTHING BUT THAT, RIGHT?

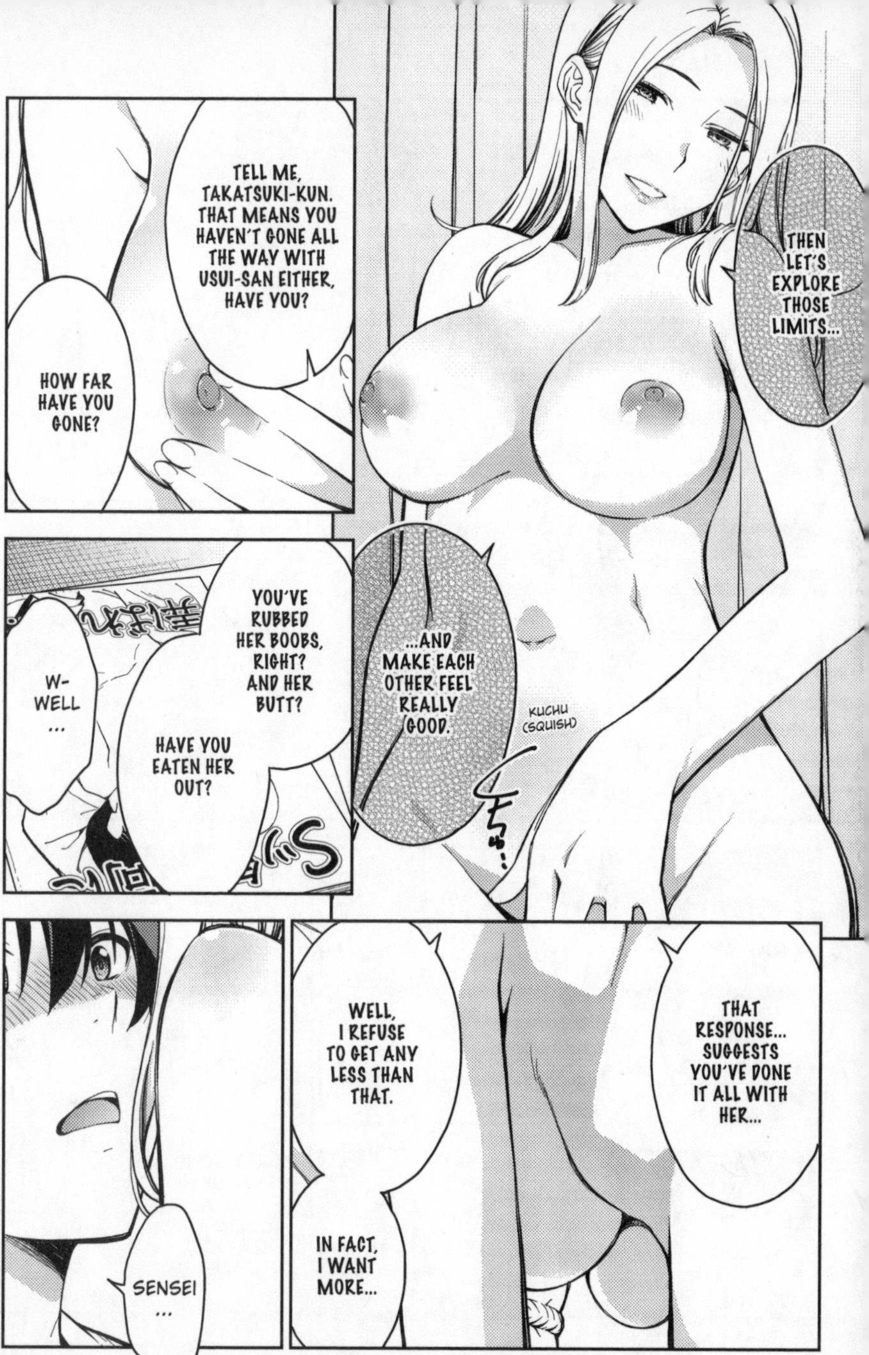
THEN LET'S EXPLORE THOSE LIMITS...
...AND MAKE EACH OTHER FEEL REALLY GOOD.
KUCHU (SQUISH)
TELL ME, TAKATSUKI-KUN. THAT MEANS YOU HAVEN'T GONE ALL THE WAY WITH USUI-SAN EITHER, HAVE YOU?
HOW FAR HAVE YOU GONE?
YOU'VE RUBBED HER BOOBS, RIGHT? AND HER BUTT?
HAVE YOU EATEN HER OUT?
W-WELL...
THAT RESPONSE... SUGGESTS YOU'VE DONE IT ALL WITH HER...
WELL, I REFUSE TO GET ANY LESS THAN THAT.
IN FACT, I WANT MORE...
SENSEI...

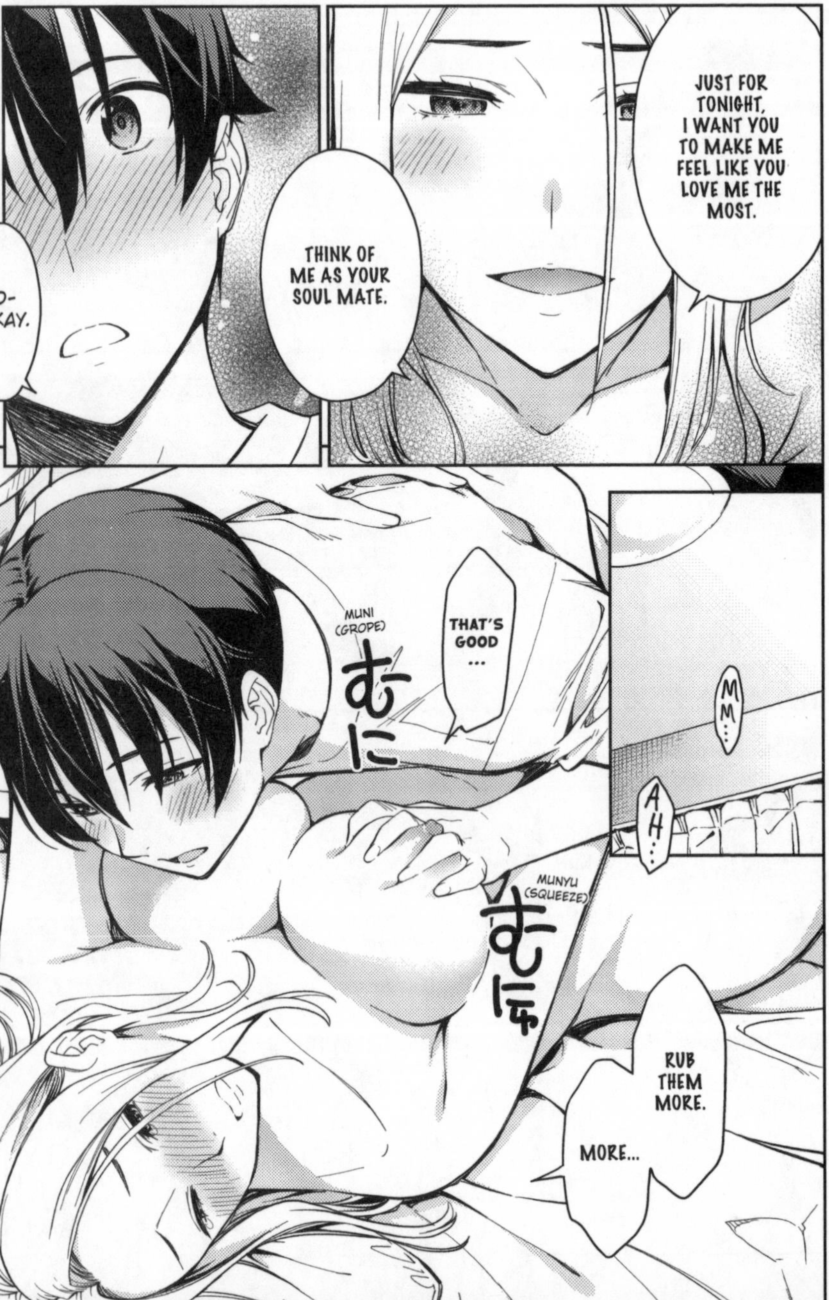
JUST FOR TONIGHT, I WANT YOU TO MAKE ME FEEL LIKE YOU LOVE ME THE MOST.
THINK OF ME AS YOUR SOUL MATE.
O-OKAY.
MM...
AH...
THAT'S GOOD...
MUNI (GROPE)
むに
MUNYU (SQUEEZE)
むにゅ
RUB THEM MORE.
MORE...

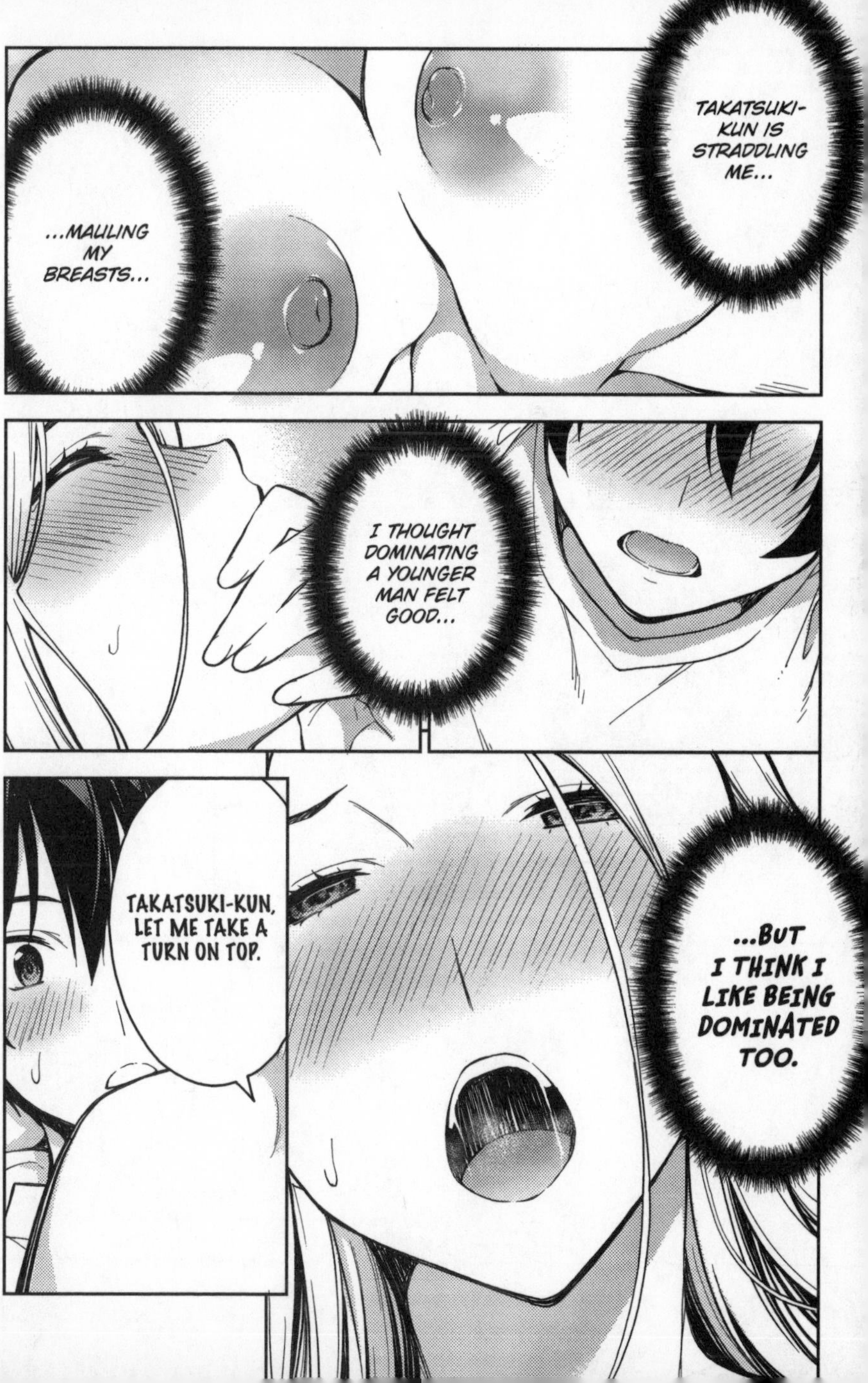
TAKATSUKI-KUN IS STRADDLING ME...
...MAULING MY BREASTS...
I THOUGHT DOMINATING A YOUNGER MAN FELT GOOD...
...BUT I THINK I LIKE BEING DOMINATED TOO.
TAKATSUKI-KUN, LET ME TAKE A TURN ON TOP.

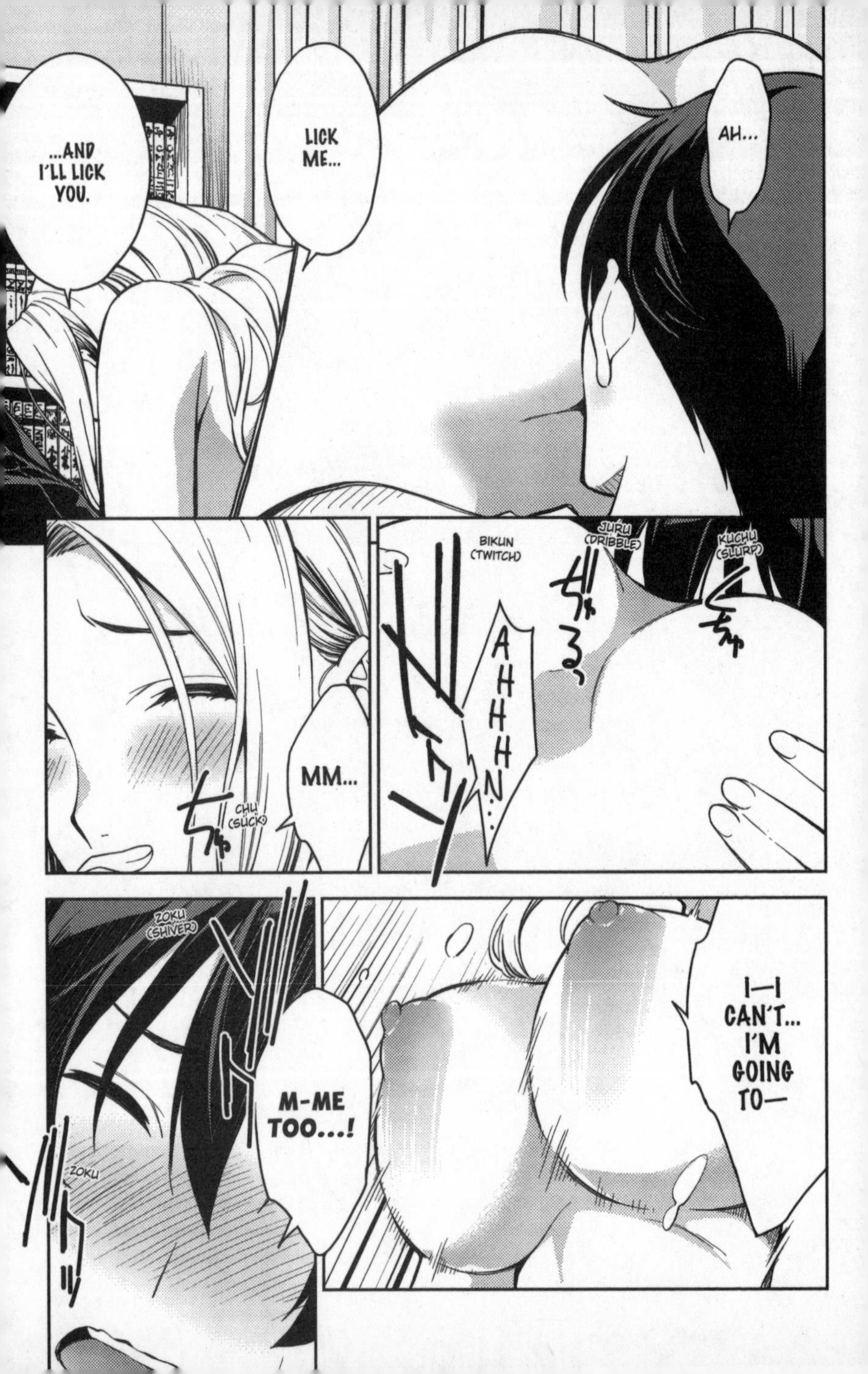
AH...
LICK ME...
...AND I'LL LICK YOU.
KUCHU (SLURP)
JURU (DRIBBLE)
BIKUN (TWITCH)
AHHHHN...
MM...
CHU (SUCK)
I—I CAN'T... I'M GOING TO—
ZOKU (SHIVER)
M-ME TOO...!
ZOKU

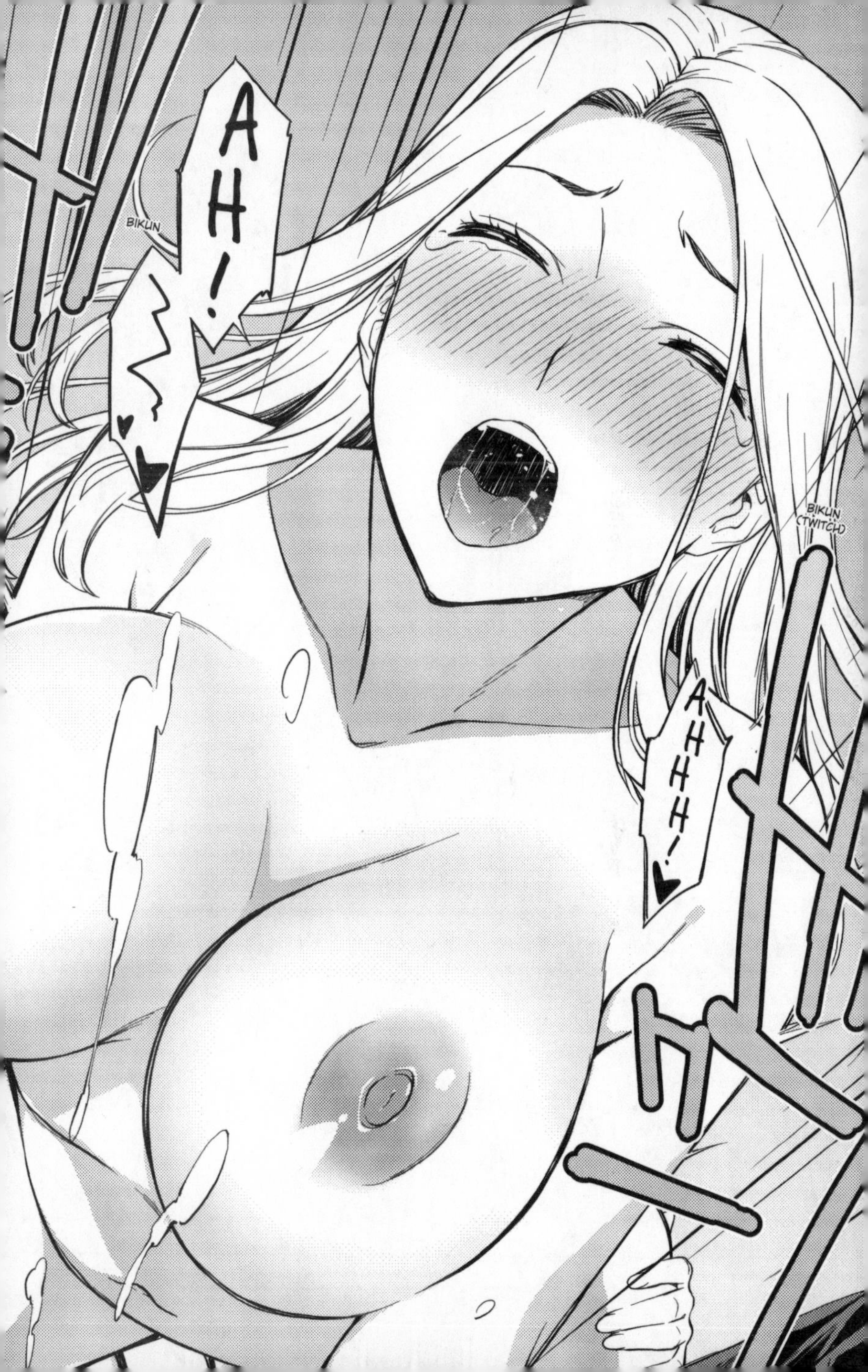
AH!
BIKUN
BIKUN (TWITCH)
AHHH!

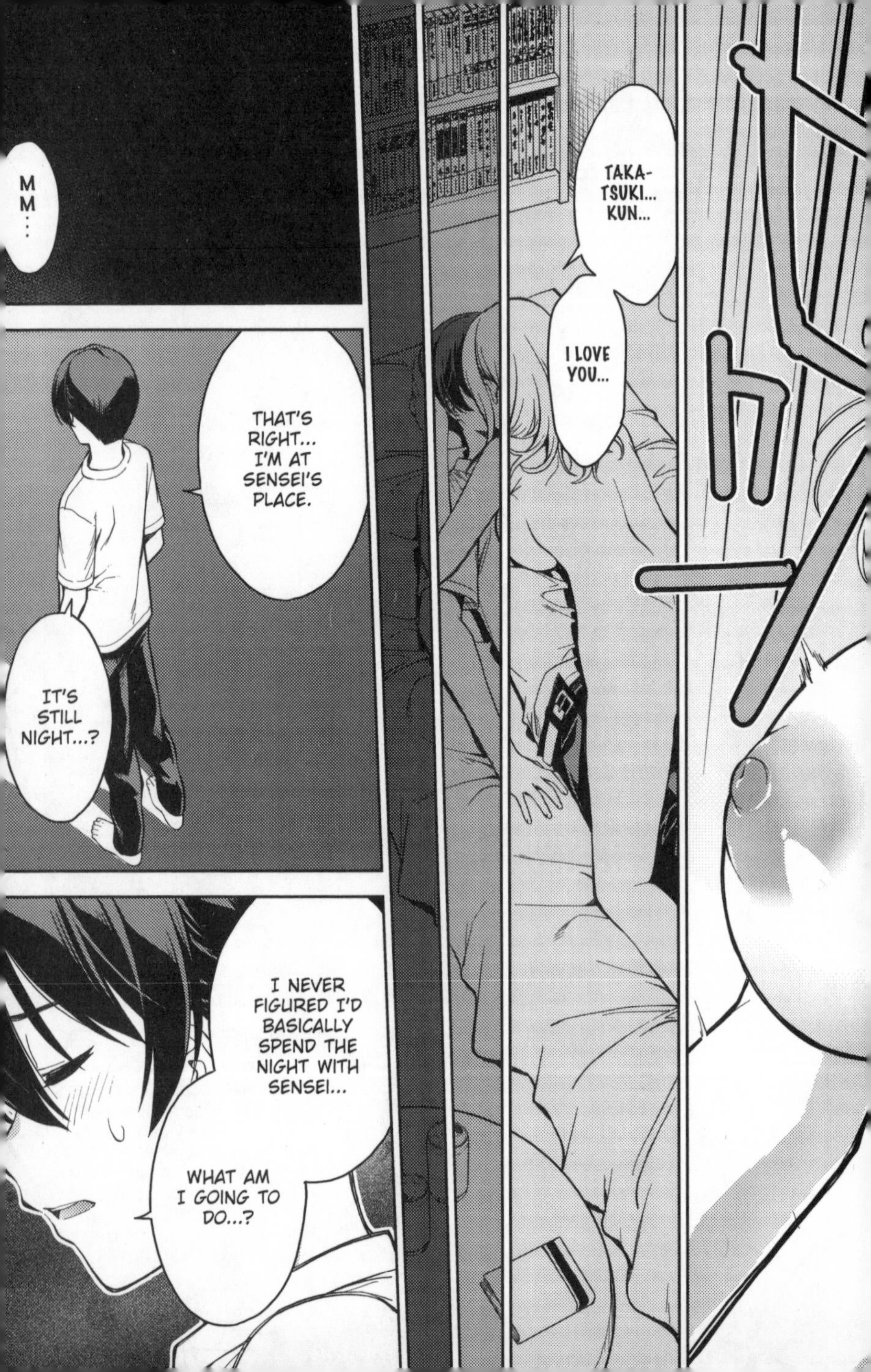
TAKA-TSUKI... KUN...
I LOVE YOU...
MM...
THAT'S RIGHT... I'M AT SENSEI'S PLACE.
IT'S STILL NIGHT...?
I NEVER FIGURED I'D BASICALLY SPEND THE NIGHT WITH SENSEI...
WHAT AM I GOING TO DO...?

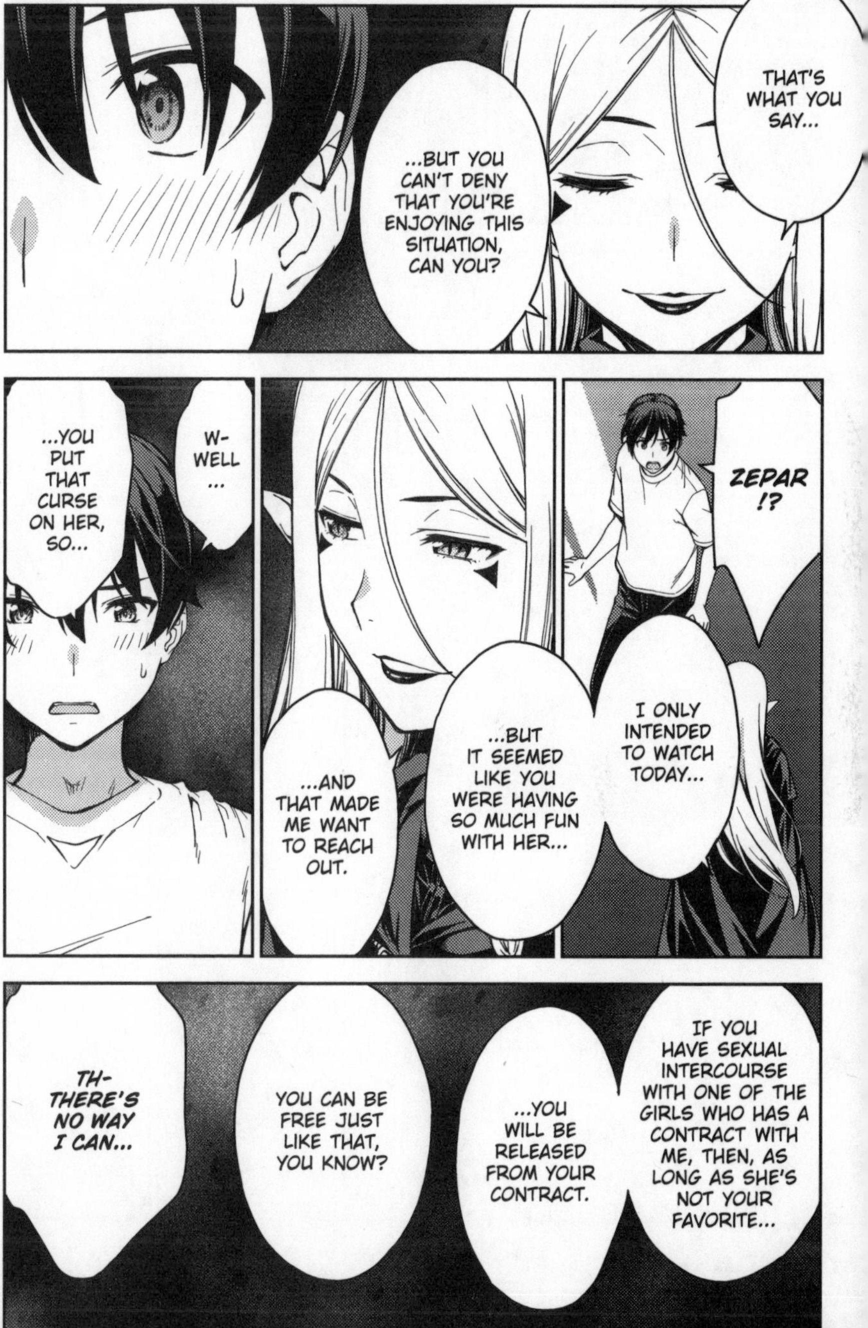
THAT'S WHAT YOU SAY...
...BUT YOU CAN'T DENY THAT YOU'RE ENJOYING THIS SITUATION, CAN YOU?
ZEPAR!?
I ONLY INTENDED TO WATCH TODAY...
...BUT IT SEEMED LIKE YOU WERE HAVING SO MUCH FUN WITH HER...
...AND THAT MADE ME WANT TO REACH OUT.
W-WELL...
...YOU PUT THAT CURSE ON HER, SO...
IF YOU HAVE SEXUAL INTERCOURSE WITH ONE OF THE GIRLS WHO HAS A CONTRACT WITH ME, THEN, AS LONG AS SHE'S NOT YOUR FAVORITE...
...YOU WILL BE RELEASED FROM YOUR CONTRACT.
YOU CAN BE FREE JUST LIKE THAT, YOU KNOW?
TH-THERE'S NO WAY I CAN...

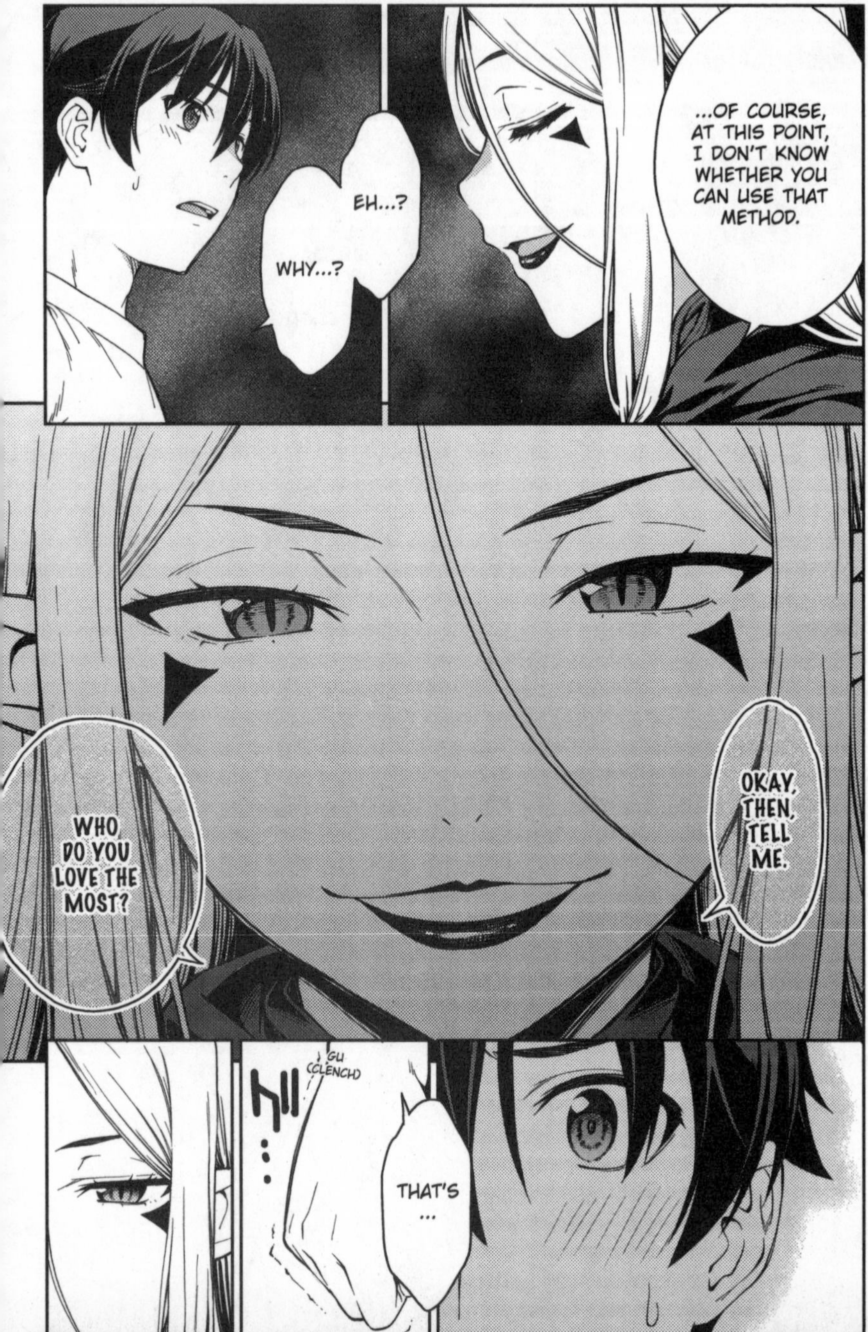
...OF COURSE, AT THIS POINT, I DON'T KNOW WHETHER YOU CAN USE THAT METHOD.
EH...?
WHY...?
OKAY, THEN, TELL ME.
WHO DO YOU LOVE THE MOST?
GU (CLENCH)
THAT'S ...

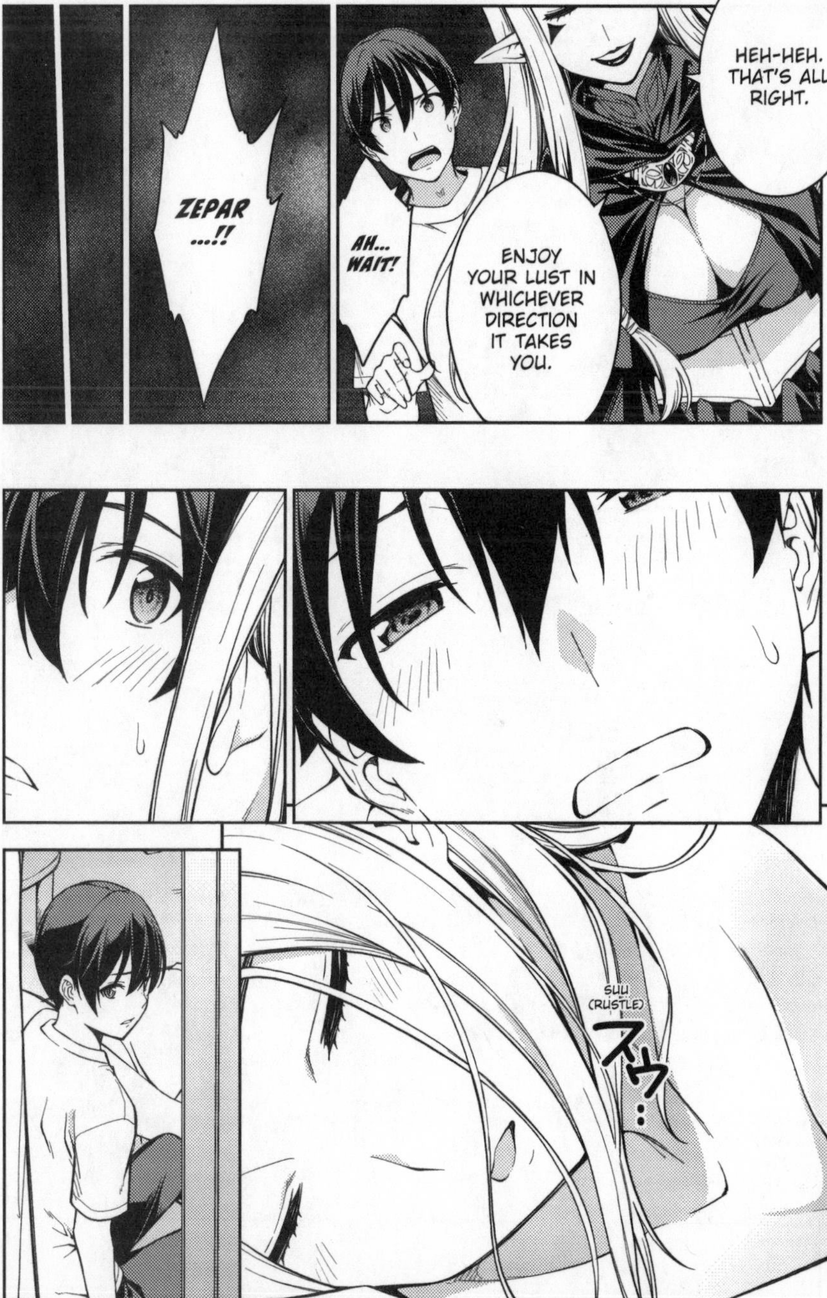
HEH-HEH. THAT'S ALL RIGHT.
ENJOY YOUR LUST IN WHICHEVER DIRECTION IT TAKES YOU.
AH... WAIT!
ZEPAR ...!!
SUU (RUSTLE)
スゥ…

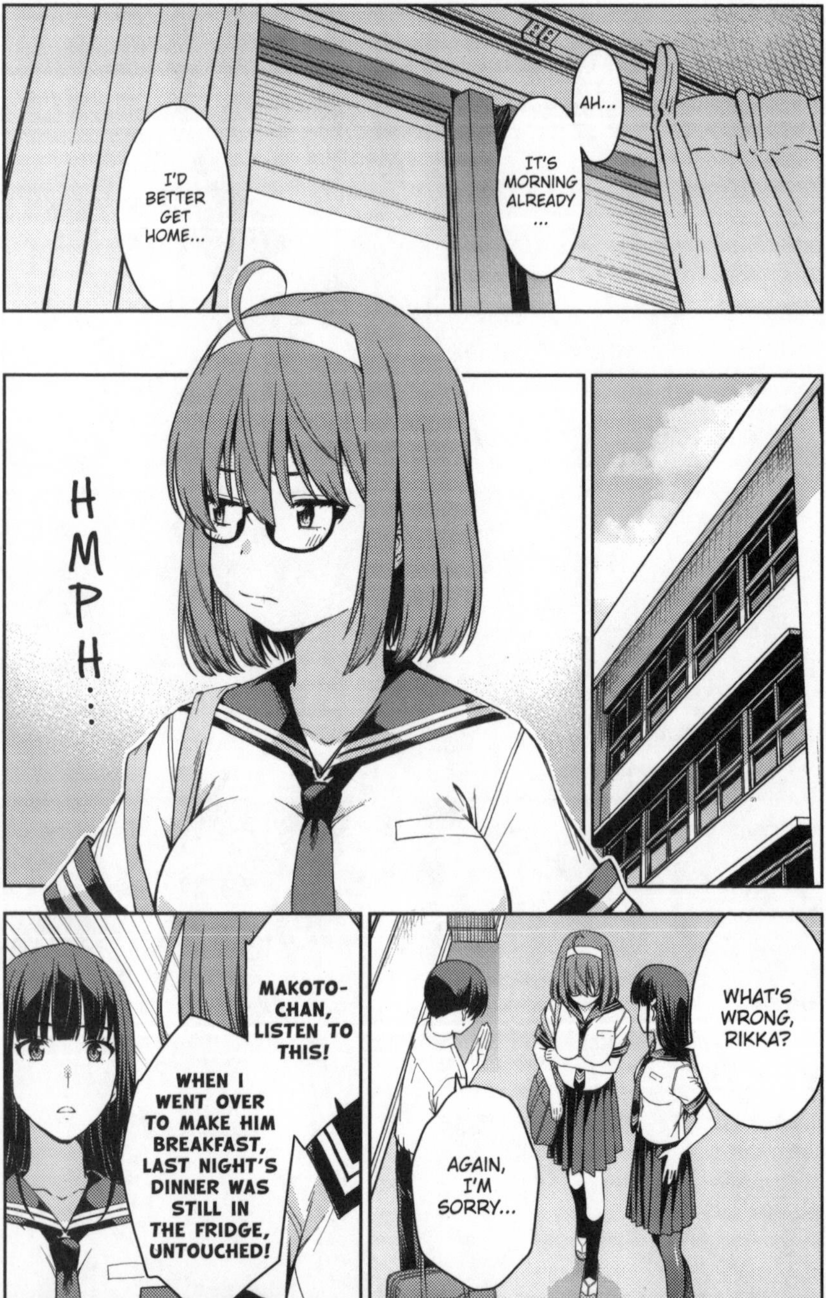
AH...
IT'S MORNING ALREADY ...
I'D BETTER GET HOME...
HMPH...
WHAT'S WRONG, RIKKA?
AGAIN, I'M SORRY...
MAKOTO-CHAN, LISTEN TO THIS!
WHEN I WENT OVER TO MAKE HIM BREAKFAST, LAST NIGHT'S DINNER WAS STILL IN THE FRIDGE, UNTOUCHED!

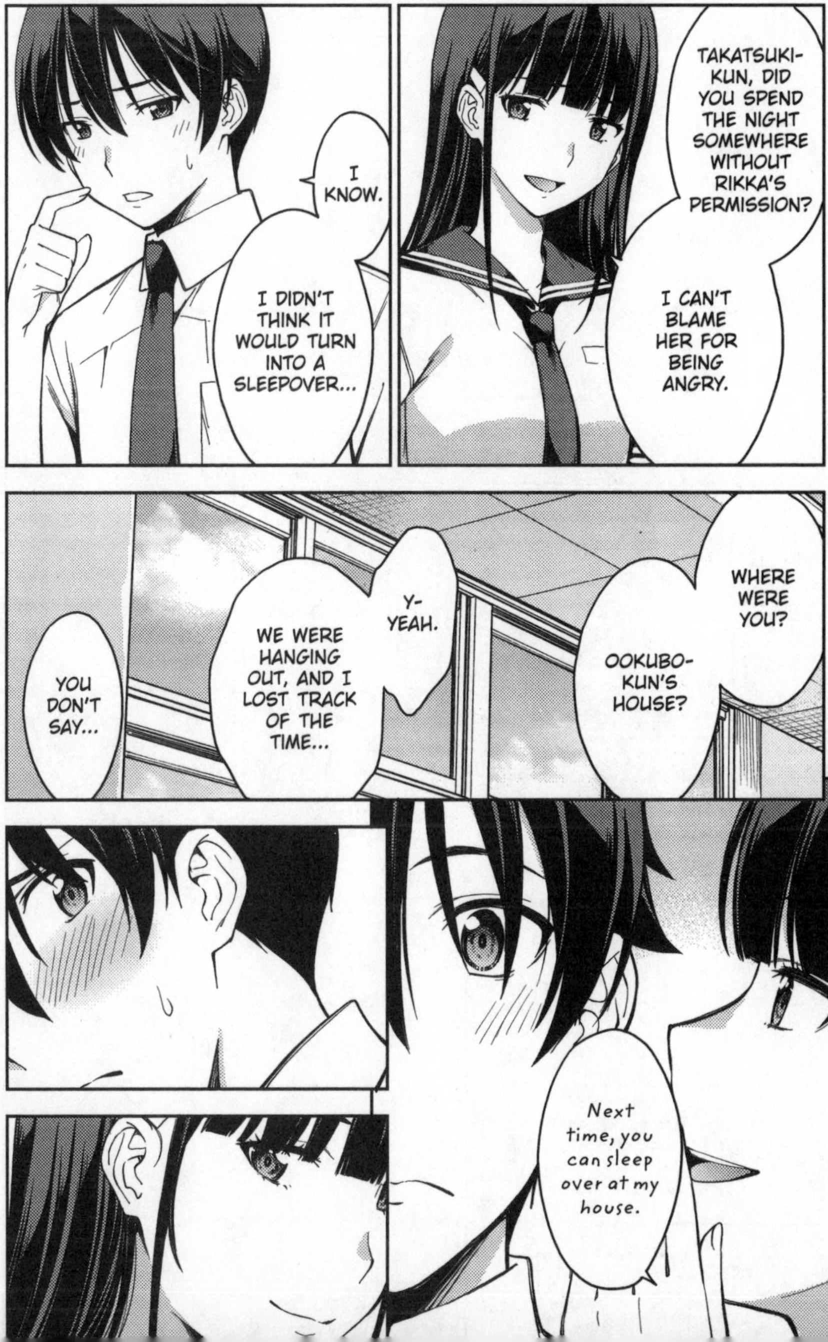
TAKATSUKI-KUN, DID YOU SPEND THE NIGHT SOMEWHERE WITHOUT RIKKA'S PERMISSION?
I CAN'T BLAME HER FOR BEING ANGRY.
I KNOW.
I DIDN'T THINK IT WOULD TURN INTO A SLEEPOVER...
WHERE WERE YOU?
OOKUBO-KUN'S HOUSE?
Y-YEAH.
WE WERE HANGING OUT, AND I LOST TRACK OF THE TIME...
YOU DON'T SAY...
Next time, you can sleep over at my house.

● Staff ●

The author
Osamu Takahashi

Assistant
Miki

Japanese edition design
Emi Nakano (BANANA GROVE STUDIO)

LUST GEASS 3

Osamu Takahashi

TRANSLATION: Sheldon Drzka • LETTERING: Phil Christie

LUST GEASS, Vol. 3
©Osamu Takahashi 2019
First published in Japan in 2019 by KADOKAWA CORPORATION, Tokyo.
English translation rights arranged with KADOKAWA CORPORATION, Tokyo through TUTTLE-MORI AGENCY, INC., Tokyo.

English translation © 2021 by Yen Press, LLC

Yen Press
150 West 30th Street, 19th Floor
New York, NY 10001

Visit us at yenpress.com • facebook.com/yenpress • twitter.com/yenpress • yenpress.tumblr.com • instagram.com/yenpress

First Yen Press Edition: March 2021

Yen Press is an imprint of Yen Press, LLC.
The Yen Press name and logo are trademarks of Yen Press, LLC.

The publisher is not responsible for websites (or their content) that are not owned by the publisher.

Library of Congress Control Number: 2020933605

ISBNs: 978-1-9753-1583-2 (paperback)
       978-1-9753-1581-8 (ebook)

10 9 8 7 6 5 4 3 2 1

WOR

Printed in the United States of America

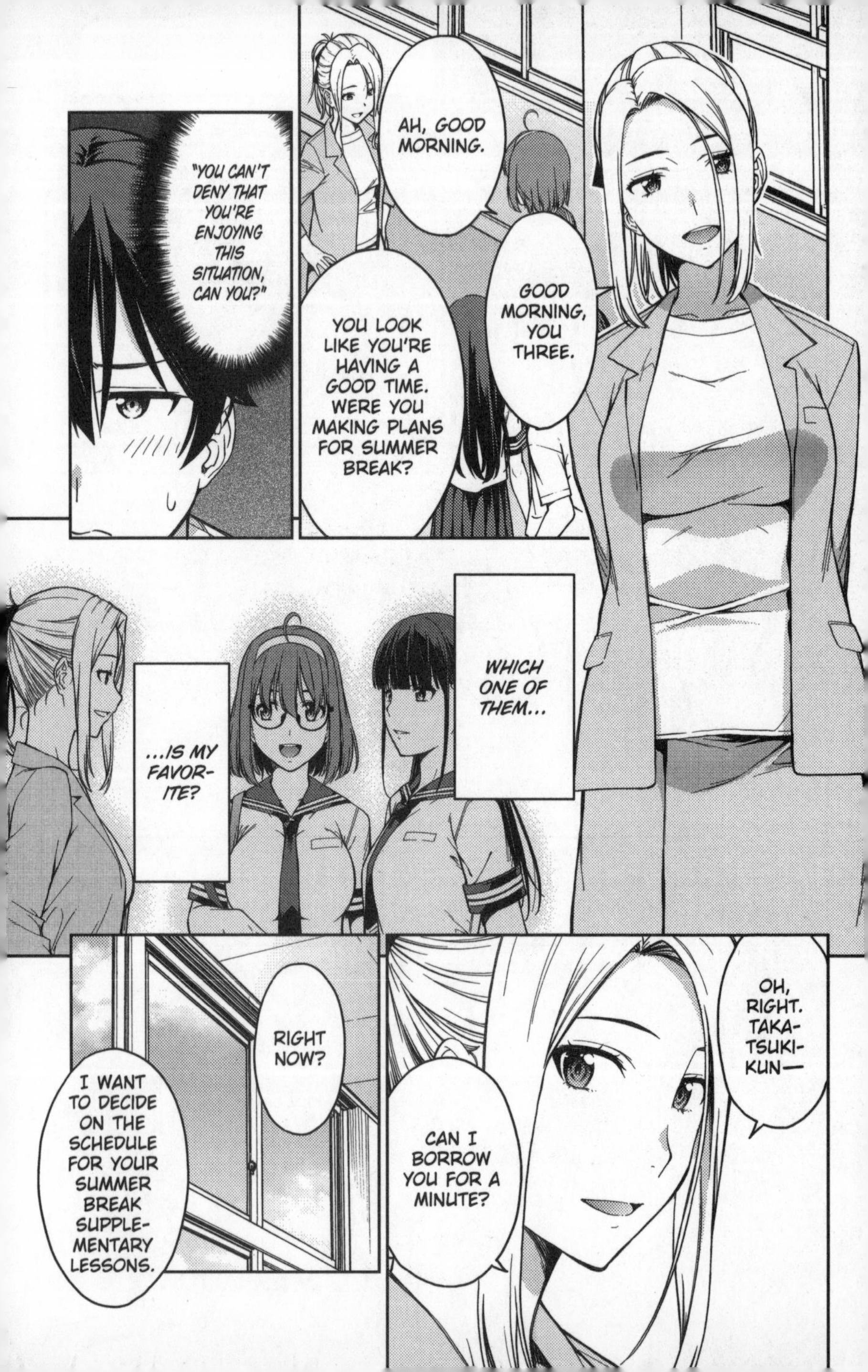
GOOD MORNING, YOU THREE.
AH, GOOD MORNING.
YOU LOOK LIKE YOU'RE HAVING A GOOD TIME. WERE YOU MAKING PLANS FOR SUMMER BREAK?
"YOU CAN'T DENY THAT YOU'RE ENJOYING THIS SITUATION, CAN YOU?"
WHICH ONE OF THEM...
...IS MY FAVOR-ITE?
OH, RIGHT. TAKA-TSUKI-KUN—
CAN I BORROW YOU FOR A MINUTE?
RIGHT NOW?
I WANT TO DECIDE ON THE SCHEDULE FOR YOUR SUMMER BREAK SUPPLE-MENTARY LESSONS.

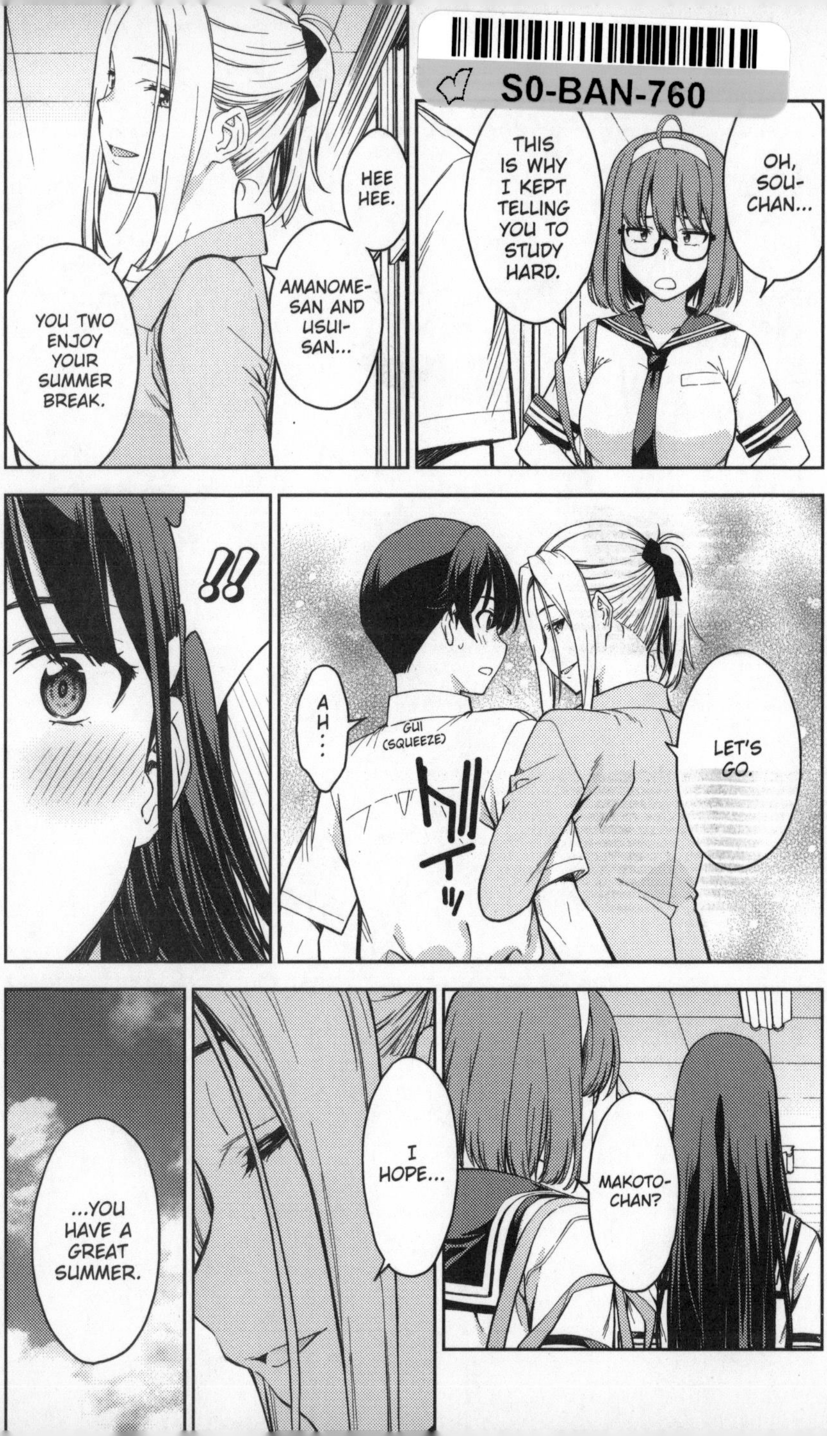
OH, SOU-CHAN...
THIS IS WHY I KEPT TELLING YOU TO STUDY HARD.
HEE HEE.
AMANOME-SAN AND USUI-SAN...
YOU TWO ENJOY YOUR SUMMER BREAK.
LET'S GO.
GUI (SQUEEZE)
AH...
!!
MAKOTO-CHAN?
I HOPE...
...YOU HAVE A GREAT SUMMER.